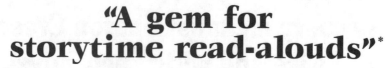

Winter 1999  The Volume 12, Number 1

New Advocate

For Those Involved with Young People and Their Literature

Published by Christopher-Gordon Publishers, Inc.
Boston

The New Advocate

Co-Editors:
Kathy G. Short and Dana L. Fox
University of Arizona

Associate Editor:
Cyndi Giorgis, University of Nevada Las Vegas

Children's Book Review Editors:
Patricia Enciso and Theresa Rogers, with Elizabeth Marshall, The Ohio State University and Christine Jenkins, University of Illinois-Champaign-Urbana

Resource Reviews:
Myra Zarnowski and Karen Patricia Smith, Queens College, CUNY

Editorial Associate:
Carmen M. Martínez-Roldán, University of Arizona, Tucson Unified School District

Editorial Assistants:
Cheri Anderson, Caryl Crowell, Stacie Cook Emert, Michele Ebersole, Debra Jacobson, Sandy Kaser, Karen Onofrey, Barbara Peterson, LaFon Phillips, Jean Schroeder, Elaine Schwartz, Tracy Smiles, and Joan Theurer, University of Arizona

Children's Voices:
Stacie Cook Emert, University of Arizona

Editorial Review Board:
Deborah W. Allen, Kean University, NJ
JoBeth Allen, University of Georgia
Bess Altwerger, Towson State University, MD
Rosalinda Barrera, University of Illinois
Rudine Sims Bishop, The Ohio State University
Randy Bomer, Queens College, CUNY
Pamela S. Carroll, Florida State University
Betty Carter, Texas Women's University
Anne Haas Dyson, University of California-Berkeley
Barbara Elleman, Marquette University
Lee Galda, University of Minnesota
Carol Gilles, University of Missouri
Yetta Goodman, University of Arizona
Marjorie R. Hancock, Kansas State University
Evelyn Hanssen, Mrachek Middle School, Denver, CO
Violet Harris, University of Illinois
Susan Hepler, Alexandria, VA
Janet Hickman, The Ohio State University
Frankey Jones, Brookwood Elementary School, Snellville, GA
Gloria Kauffman, Duffy Elementary School, Tucson, AZ
Patricia C. McKissack, Chesterfield, MO
Diana Mitchell, Michigan State University
Elizabeth Noll, University of New Mexico
Kathryn Mitchell Pierce, Glenridge Elementary School, Clayton, MO
Karen Smith, National Council of Teachers of English

J. Kevin Spink, Mt. View School, Anchorage, AK
Joel Taxel, University of Georgia
Ann Trousdale, Louisiana State University
Richard Van Dongen, University of New Mexico
Lauren L. Wohl, Hyperion Books for Children
JoAnn Wong-Kam, Punahou School, Honolulu, HI
Junko Yokota, National-Louis University, Chicago, IL
Jane Yolen, Hatfield, MA

For the Volume 12 cover illustration, David Diaz drew the sketch on watercolor paper then inked and painted it using watercolor, gouache, and dyes. He hopes his illustration will represent "the importance of reading" to the audience of *The New Advocate*.

All photos © Joel Brown and used with permission.

Manuscripts and editorial correspondence should be sent to: Kathy G. Short and Dana L. Fox, 515 College of Education, University of Arizona, Tucson, AZ 85721.

The Advocates of Literature for Young People Board of Directors

Carol J. Fisher, Department of Language Education, University of Georgia, Athens, GA 30602

Southeast Region: Linda DeGroff, Department of Language Education, The University of Georgia, Athens, GA 30602
Northeast Region: Joan Glazer, Horace Mann #212, Rhode Island College, Providence, RI 02908
Midwest Region: Violet Harris, Curriculum and Instruction, University of Illinois, Champaign, IL 61820
Far West Region: Patricia Lyons, Department of Education, California State University, Chico, CA 95929

The New Advocate is published by Christopher-Gordon Publishers, Inc., 1502 Providence Highway, Suite 12, Norwood, MA 02062 four times a year, in December, March, June, and September. Subscription rates are $30.00 prepaid; $45.00 for purchase orders. Add $10.00 per year for Canadian and all other international postage. Single copies are available for $10.00, prepaid, plus $1 for shipping and handling.

Remittances should be made payable to *The New Advocate* by check, money order, or bank draft in United States currency. Communication regarding orders, subscriptions, single copies, advertising, change of address, and permission to reprint should be addressed to *The New Advocate*, 1502 Providence Highway, Suite 12, Norwood, MA 02062, (781-762-5577. Copyright © 1998 by Christopher-Gordon Publishers, Inc. ISSN: 0895-1381.

All claims regarding duplicate or missing copies must be made within 30 days of the last day of an issue's publication month.

Table of Contents

Volume 12, Number 1, Winter 1999

Teaching Reading within a Literature-Based Curriculum: Notes from the Co-Editors

Dana L. Fox and Kathy G. Short

Just a few years ago, educators who valued literature's powerful role in children's lives were riding a wave of success. Libraries and classrooms were overflowing with more high-quality books than ever before. Literature had become more than just another way to teach reading; literature, valued as a way of knowing, was woven into every aspect of the curriculum. However, the world looks very different now as politicians and the media call for systematic, intensive phonics instruction and decodable texts. Literature is once again a "frill" reserved for students who finish their "real" work early or for those students who reach a certain reading level.

Despite this political backlash, we know that many educators persist in bringing students and books together because they believe that literature remains a powerful force both in the teaching of reading and in children's lives. Themed issues are not typical for *The New Advocate*; however, because of the current political context facing educators, we decided to focus one issue of the journal on this important topic. We posed the following questions as points of departure for this themed issue of *The New Advocate*:

- How do educators support students in becoming proficient readers with effective reading strategies within a literature-based curriculum?
- Can books be used to teach reading strategies without ruining the literary experience?
- What is the role of skills within such a curriculum?
- How do educators use literature to support students who are struggling? How do educators adapt to a wider range of student abilities?
- What does it mean to "balance" strategy instruction with literature?

Articles in this issue of *The New Advocate* demonstrate that teaching reading is not an "either/or" issue nor is eclecticism the answer. Instead, educators show how teachers can teach reading skills and strategies and still keep the primary focus on meaning:

Nicholasa Mohr reflects upon how she learned to read and how reading gave her a sense of freedom and pride in her own Puerto Rican heritage.

Randy Bomer discusses how we might use reading conferences to assist upper grade students who struggle with reading.

Heidi Mills with **Tim O'Keefe** explores the stance of the teacher in the teaching of reading within a literature-based classroom.

Carol Gilles with **Jean Dickinson** outlines the difference between "drilling for skills" and "becoming skillful readers" and shows how teachers can help students become skillful readers, writers, discussants, and thinkers through literature discussion.

Kathy Quick describes how she teaches comprehension strategies to reluctant readers through literature study.

Pat Scharer discusses how teachers, supervisors, and administrators can form a partnership to create a unified response to the concerns of parents and legislators.

We are also pleased to welcome new editors for our children's literature and professional resources review columns. **Patricia Enciso** and **Theresa Rogers** of The Ohio State University along with **Elizabeth Marshall** of The Ohio State University and **Christine Jenkins** of University of Illinois-Champaign-Urbana will co-edit "Connecting Children with Literature in Classrooms and Communities." Their column will pair recent books with landmark books and will be organized around themes such as social action, identity, and gender. They will work closely with a team of classroom teachers from kindergarten through middle school as well as parents and community members.

Myra Zarnowski and **Karen Patricia Smith** of Queens College, City University of New York, will co-edit "Connecting Educators with Professional Resources." Their column will help readers learn about recent resources for curriculum planning and literature study and will be organized around themes such as teaching with nonfiction, the art of storytelling, and dealing with controversial issues.

To introduce our cover illustration for Volume 12 of *The New Advocate*, **Cyndi Giorgis** opens this issue with her conversation with David and Cecelia Diaz about the "business" of illustrating children's books and David's process as an artist. As always, we welcome your comments and suggestions related to any article or feature in this issue of *The New Advocate*.

It's All about the Process:
Talking with David and Cecelia Diaz

Cyndi Giorgis

David Diaz seemed to burst onto the children's book publishing scene when he received the 1995 Caldecott Award for his first illustrated book. However, prior to the Caldecott, David had done covers for numerous books and had also operated his own successful illustration/ design business with his wife, Cecelia. A few months ago, I was fortunate to be able to spend the afternoon talking with David and Cecelia in their studio located near their home in San Diego. David and Cecelia are both very warm and friendly and immediately made me feel welcome as they took me on a tour of their studio, and later, their home. The focus of our discussion that afternoon was on David's process of illustrating as well as the excitement leading up to his receiving the 1995 Caldecott Award for his illustrations in *Smoky Night*, a book about the Los Angeles riots. The rest of our conversation centered on David's various artistic pursuits, which include creating illustrations for his business and for children's picture books.

A Collaborative Process

David and Cecelia run their business, Diaz Icon, from their studio, which is actually a second house they have recently purchased. This house has allowed them to create a studio in a home-like atmosphere. On tables downstairs

Cyndi Giorgis is an Assistant Professor in Instructional and Curricular Studies at the University of Nevada Las Vegas. She is Associate Editor of *The New Advocate*.

David illustrated four picture books, which he felt was too many. The next year he completed one book and then, in 1997, he illustrated three. David comments, "Three seems about right, where I do one book each spring and then two in the fall. It seems that as soon as I'm done with one, there's another looming on the horizon."

A children's book illustrator who has influenced David's thinking about his work is William Steig. Steig works in a simple line style using watercolor and pen-and-ink, a style that seems to be distinctly different from David's. But the connection resulted from what Steig was able to accomplish through his artwork rather than the style itself. David remembers, "I had no idea at first who William Steig was. I'd seen *The New Yorker* as much as anybody else, but I hadn't paid close attention to his work. One day, I was looking in a used bookstore and found a copy of his book, *Male and Female*. I was amazed by how much was going on in his small sketchy drawings that conveyed so much feeling and humor. Seeing his work just really affected me. I was at the point where I was starting off illustrating and doing a lot of emulation, where you look closely at other people's work over time in order to experiment with other techniques and try to reinterpret it in order to find your own style. So I saw that book and I was trying to figure out, what is it that I do. I think every illustrator goes through this process where you're trying to figure out what your voice is. How do you draw? How do you write? I did a lot of experimenting. So when I saw his book, I became interested in his work. Then I started looking for his work in the library and trying to see more of what he did. I got one of the old collections of his work. It was funny stuff, but it was very drawn and articulated. I drew a parallel between what he did and where I was with my background in the super-realist movement. I thought, what's really important here is the essence of what's there, not just the technique. Finding his work was great because I saw how William created over time. His work got so much better as he moved away from tight lines and got looser and more relaxed. I found that the same thing happened in my work. My lines were much tighter in *Smoky Night* than they are now. I actually spoke with Steig one day and had a sweet conversation with him. I think he's done illustrating books. He's in his nineties. When I spoke to him, he said he just finished his last book. I hope it's not his last book. I'd love to be ninety and still be illustrating."

Sharing the Process with Children

When David speaks to children and draws for them, he wants them to understand that drawing is not complicated. "When I draw, I break it down into the simplest forms and just go through the steps of making a picture—eyes are football shaped, the mouth is an 'm' shape, ears are the handle on the mug—just really simple to show them that it's no more complicated than that. They understand that it's not a big deal to draw and it really isn't. There's no mystery to it. You just have to do it." David was encouraged to develop his own art talents when he was younger, but his parents advised him to do something else "as a backup."

David and Cecelia were recently invited to Abilene, Texas where David had the opportunity to exhibit his work at the National Center for Children's

Illustrated Literature. While there, David was asked to speak about his artwork to several large groups of children. During the presentations, Cecelia sat in the audience worrying because she thought he was losing the almost two thousand second graders who, at one point, seemed to be paying little attention. However, several weeks later David and Cecelia received a book from the second graders in Abilene containing what Cecelia called "unbelievable images." Both Cecelia and David were surprised that what they perceived as a lack of attention on the part of the children was actually not the case at all. Cecelia's voice reflected her amazement, "The kids took what David was doing and went inside of themselves to create these wonderful images with the simple techniques that David had shown them."

David and Cecelia, like many parents, are concerned that funding for fine arts is being eliminated in the public school system and that children may not have the opportunity to experience art. Cecelia feels that too often schools focus on subjects such as math and English while ignoring other areas such as art and music. "It's really a shame that the whole curriculum is just pegging kids into two different subjects. And the only art classes they have in schools are the after school activities that parents pay for. It's a pity and the kids are so frustrated. Our middle son feels that way because they never do art in class. He loves art. He's a very passionate, artistic person. We're going to lose kids completely the way our school system is right now."

Caldecott Award Process

The Randolph Caldecott Medal has been awarded annually since 1938 to the artist who creates the most distinguished book illustrated for children during the preceding year. David Diaz was awarded the 1995 Caldecott Award for his illustrations in *Smoky Night*. Even though *Smoky Night* was David's first picture book, he is quick to point out that he had been illustrating for over 12 years prior to receiving the award. However, receiving the prestigious Caldecott medal as a newcomer to the world of children's picture books is rather uncommon. Most recipients have illustrated numerous children's books and are well-known in the field. David Diaz's unique style of art captured the attention of the Caldecott Award committee and gained him recognition early in this aspect of his career. As with his art, David feels that his success in the children's book publishing industry was a result of sowing seeds. He did not initially set out to illustrate children's books but an editor saw a poster he had created and contacted him about illustrating *Neighborhood Odes*. He then began working to "break into" the field. "You send out promotional material, call people and get people to see your work. It takes awhile to get established. And you wonder if they will like your work and hope they'll send you a project."

Cecelia has been an active observer in this process over the years. She commented, "David was still sowing the seeds before the Caldecott was announced. He had a proposal for a book with an editor and he had been waiting for about six months. When the Caldecott was announced, there was a deal on the table from the editor right away. That was the difference between receiving a Caldecott as opposed to being an illustrator who is working hard, knocking on doors and saying, this is my work. At first, no one is listening because they have all these other people with awards they are already working with. When David received the Caldecott, that moment crystallized everything and all of a sudden we had flowers arriving at the door and everybody wanted to talk to him. But at the same time, it wasn't just that easy because David has worked really hard. Thank God for the people who looked at *Smoky Night* and said that there was something really unique about this particular book."

> *I know it seems unbelievable to some illustrators, but each book I do will be one that I have illustrated, designed and created a typeface for.*

Even though the Newbery and Caldecott Award recipients are generally announced in January or February, the awards are not handed out until the banquet held during the summer conference of the American Library Association. This banquet is attended by well over a thousand people and the Newbery and Caldecott Award winners are asked to speak. David and Cecelia went to New York for a vacation before the conference that was held in Chicago in 1995. David felt he made a mistake in attempting to take a vacation before the banquet because he thought about nothing else but his speech the entire time he was in New York. David's style of speaking is also unique because, as he tells it, "I had only two index cards with key words on them and I just kind of flowed with it because I feel more comfortable just speaking rather than reading a speech. There are some writers who read their speech word for word and they speak beautifully. It was a whole new world for me." After the stressful banquet was over, David was ready for a vacation, but unfortunately he and Cecelia had to head home to California and back to work.

The process of selecting the Caldecott Award is a fascinating one for David. "It's interesting that the Caldecott artwork is judged by literature people, whereas the opposite would be illustrators judging text. Not to say that it's wrong because it's judged on its relevance to children's literature, but in some ways it's interesting that, with Caldecott, you're addressing primarily literature people and a great importance is placed on the writing as well as the illustrations."

Impact of the Literary Review Process of Children's Books

David has illustrated numerous books since receiving the Caldecott Award. Several of these books have dealt with societal issues, such as homelessness in the book *December* written by Eve Bunting. Cecelia and David both agree that these books are not "bedtime books," but are very important in providing children with an opportunity to discuss issues that they may deal with every day. In the publishing industry, book reviews that appear in numerous professional journals and magazines in the fields of library science, education, journalism, and so on influence individuals who write, illustrate, edit, publish, purchase and share books for and with children. *Just One Flick of a Finger* by Marybeth Lorbiecki and illustrated by David Diaz focuses on the issue of teenagers and guns. David says, "The book received mixed reviews and subsequently didn't do very well. It's one of my favorite books because it's such a timely topic. I think there are cases where reviews actually hinder an important book from getting out there." Cecelia also feels strongly that *Just One Flick of a Finger* addresses an important issue in today's society, especially with the number of teenagers bringing guns to school and shooting fellow classmates or teachers. Every day she cuts out newspaper articles dealing with this topic as a reminder that issues such as these must be addressed in children's books.

Even though *Just One Flick of a Finger* was not reviewed well, David still believes that reviews are important. "Thousands of children's books are published each year and you need someone to guide and direct you. Sometimes I think I've created a certain look with what I'm trying to accomplish with my books and it's different than 95 percent of what other illustrators are doing. *Smoky Night* was out for a year before the Caldecott was announced and it was doing okay. It had several starred reviews in the review journals, but at times it would get a controversial review. The real controversy happened after the Caldecott Award, which caused the book to be re-examined. But the reviews are important and of course you're going to like the reviews that are accurate or favorable and not like the ones that are unfavorable."

There are also times when a reviewer appears to have an incomplete understanding of the work David does as an artist. Once a reviewer referred to David as "a one-man design circus." David enjoys creating "a complete statement" for the books he illustrates. "I look at it beyond being 'just' an illustrator in that I am not only making pictures for books but I am creating a visual vocabulary and providing a complete balance between text, image, and design. I have a design background where I am allowed to do what I want to do and to have control or at least the illusion of complete control of what I am doing." David also seems to have an understanding of how children respond to his books. "Kids, unlike many adults, will spend time looking at the book, and I know that the more engaging the total look is, then the more time they'll spend and the greater the book experience will become." Both Cecelia and David agree that "everybody has a right to an opinion, but not everybody sees things the same way. Not everybody can read one book and get to the same message."

Evolution of the Process

In looking at the illustrations David Diaz has created for *Smoky Night, Just One Flick of a Finger, December, Wilma Unlimited* and *Going Home*, it might be perceived that there is one style that is characteristically "David Diaz." However, his most recent books, *The Little Scarecrow Boy* and *The Disappearing Alphabet*, both to be published in fall 1998, and *Jump Rope Magic*, to be published in Spring 1999, are a definite departure from his previous style. These books, like all of his others, have proceeded through the process of conceptualizing, imagining, and seeing what works with the manuscript. David describes *The Little Scarecrow Boy* as "very sweet"—a term that probably would not be used with his previous illustrations. David admits that there was a conscious effort to change his style with *The Little Scarecrow Boy*. "I did a couple of sketches when I was doing my preliminary work and I'm thinking this could work, but I would really like to do something different. The story is very traditional. It's really sweet. It's light. The artwork couldn't be too heavy-handed for the manuscript. That's what pushed me to try another style." This style involves creating round, adorable faces of scarecrows done in watercolors of light blue and yellow.

Even though *The Little Scarecrow Boy* is dramatically different from his previous illustrations, David insists that "the process is always evolving. Each book is still from within a part of me. The illustrations for *The Disappearing Alphabet* are done in the style that I've been doing for years from my regular editorial days. But it's the first time that it will be seen in a picture book because the book works well in that style." Cecelia agrees that it's not another style but rather is one that is contained within the scope of David's work.

Cecelia and their three children often play an active role in the process as a picture book evolves. When David was working on *The Little Scarecrow Boy*, he would leave the paintings on the table in their home each night and, in the morning, the children would eagerly look forward to "seeing what Daddy drew." Cecelia and the children would reread the story with the new accompanying illustrations. But even though David has his own live-in critics, he insists he would not change his artwork. He feels he has a sense of where each painting is going and the concept of the book overall.

Part of the process for many illustrators is the move toward writing their own books as well. David thinks that writing "is the scariest thing in the world. I'm sure that, to a writer, illustrating could seem just as daunting. But I do read a lot and I think that is part of what it takes to write. I would never assume that just because I received the Caldecott that now I'm going to write a book. I don't take it that lightly. I know there are responsibilities in writing." David will be taking these responsibilities seriously in the near future, because he has a contract to write and illustrate a book in the coming year.

Process of Creating the Cover for *The New Advocate*

David begins every illustration by trying to figure out what will work best for that particular project and "client." For *The New Advocate*, it was necessary for David to get a sense of the journal and the focus of the articles published. The first thing David did was to look at *The New Advocate* to understand the ideas that were being conveyed to the readers. David knew that he wanted to project the idea of books and reading and the importance of both. His process of conceptualizing, imagining, and seeing what works was employed here as well.

Initially, David did five different sketches using the styles found in *Smoky Night* as well as *The Little Scarecrow Boy*. These sketches were then sent to the publishers of *The New Advocate* as well as to the co-editors and associate editor. The sketch selected was the one that conveyed the idea of books and reading and really spoke to us through its style. David then drew the sketch on watercolor paper, then inked and painted it using watercolor, gouache and dyes. David's hope is that this illustration will represent the idea of "the importance of reading" to the audience of *The New Advocate*. David believes the readers of

The New Advocate are those individuals who are knowledgeable about children's literature as well as about effective ways to use it for sharing with children. "I believe that these are some of the same people who helped *Smoky Night* earn the Caldecott Award, because they are the ones who are using and sharing literature with children in the classroom." David feels that *The New Advocate* reaches those individuals who are concerned not only about children's literacy development, but also about using literature through a "hands-on approach."

It Really Is All About the Process

David understands and looks forward to his continued evolution as a children's book illustrator. "I want to keep evolving because, as I have probably said a thousand times, it's all about the process and the process keeps evolving over time. The correlation I make is that how you are teaching now is probably completely different than it was last year, but it's evolved from when you began teaching. You get better. You teach smarter. You write smarter. You eliminate a lot of the false starts that you've had in the past. And no matter what your career is, the more you do it, the better and more 'efficient you are. And that's what it's about. The work I did eighteen years ago was great, but now I think it's even better. So when I'm taking on an assignment, I try to think 'What's an appropriate solution to this manuscript?' and sometimes it might be similar to what I've done before, and sometimes it's not. Probably, the most dramatic change is *The Little Scarecrow Boy*, which is done in watercolor and pencil. Then my next book after that, *Jump Rope Magic*, is an evolution from *The Little Scarecrow Boy*. It's the next step away. I hope that my work does keep evolving, because it really is all about the process."

Books Illustrated by David Diaz

Brown, M. W. (1998). *The little scarecrow boy*. Ill. D. Diaz. New York: HarperCollins.

Bunting, E. (1994). *Smoky night*. Ill. D. Diaz. San Diego, CA: Harcourt Brace.

Bunting, E. (1996). *Going home*. Ill. D. Diaz. New York: HarperCollins.

Bunting, E. (1997). *December*. Ill. D. Diaz. San Diego, CA: Harcourt Brace.

Kimmel, E. A. (1998). *Be not far from me: The oldest love story: Legends from the Bible*. Ill. D. Diaz. New York: Simon & Schuster.

Krull, K. (1996). *Wilma unlimited: How Wilma Rudolph became the world's fastest woman*. Ill. D. Diaz. San Diego, CA: Harcourt Brace.

Lorbiecki, M. (1996). *Just one flick of a finger*. Ill. D. Diaz. New York: Dial.

Merriam, E. (1996). *The inner city Mother Goose*. Ill. D. Diaz. New York: Simon & Schuster.

Scruggs, A. (1999). *Jump rope magic*. Ill. D. Diaz. New York: Scholastic.

Soto, G. (1992). *Neighborhood odes*. Ill. D. Diaz. San Diego, CA: Harcourt Brace.

Wilbur, R. (1998). *The disappearing alphabet*. Ill. D. Diaz. San Diego, CA: Harcourt Brace.

The New Advocate

The Premier Journal for All Those Concerned with Young People and Their Literature

Special Call for Classroom Vignettes

Learning through Story

Story is the very stuff of teaching, the landscape within which we live as teachers . . . and within which the work of teachers can be seen as making sense. (Freema Elbaz, 1990)

As Co-Editors of *The New Advocate*, we invite teachers and others directly involved in schools to write brief stories about their students' engagements with literature in the classroom. Such narratives, we believe, may help us organize the complexity of our experience into a body of practical knowledge. We are interested in success stories as well as stories that convey the uncertainties and misgivings that are an everyday part of teachers' lives. We seek stories that illustrate lessons learned and those that represent unresolved issues or dilemmas related to literature in the classroom. These stories may take the form of profiles of individual students, accounts of small groups or entire classes, or teachers' autobiographical reflections.

At least one vignette will be published in each issue of *The New Advocate* in a section in the journal entitled, "Learning through Story." Any classroom teacher who has a vignette published in *The New Advocate* will receive a $75.00 grant for professional books from Christopher-Gordon Publishers, Inc.

Manuscript deadlines (1998–1999):
August 1, November 1, February 1, and May 1,

Manuscript Guidelines. Vignettes generally should not exceed 2–4 double-spaced, typed pages. APA style is preferred. Decisions about all articles are made within two to three months of submission. Include a cover sheet with the author's name, affiliation, position, preferred mailing address, telephone number(s), and FAX number. The author's name should not appear on the manuscript. Please submit four (4) copies and two (2) self-addressed, stamped envelopes to:

Dana L. Fox and Kathy G. Short, Co-Editors
The New Advocate
Department of Language, Reading and Culture
515 College of Education
University of Arizona
Tucson, Arizona 85721

Freedom to Read

Nicholasa Mohr

It would benefit educators to reflect and ask the question, "Who is the average American child, or teenager? Who is it that we are supposed to educate?" The young people who fill our schools in urban America and in many rural areas are not only White or middle class. They do not always live in a two-parent home with a lovely backyard in an ideal neighborhood.

I know because I was such a child who did not fit into the stereotype of the so-called "average" American girl.

I grew up in these United States, a daughter of the Puerto Rican Diaspora, born and raised in the barrios of urban America located in the heart of New York City. Back then, in the 1940s and '50s, I was unaware that throughout the United States there were many other barrios similar to my own. I had no idea that Latino culture existed beyond the East Coast and was spread out among large populations of Hispanics living in cities such as Chicago, Tampa, San Antonio, or Los Angeles. Just like my family, those Hispanic Americans spoke both Spanish and English, shopped in the bodegas, ate plantains with rice and beans, listened to the Spanish radio programs, and attended Mass in Spanish. I imagine that many of those children, like the youngsters in my barrio, might have even attempted to read our parents' copy of the Spanish language daily newspapers.

Nicholasa Mohr is a writer of children's, young adult, and adult literature. She received the Hispanic Heritage Award for Literature in 1997.

However, beyond a particular ethnic identity, we Latino children also shared a commonality of culture with all other American youngsters throughout our nation. For example, at home, we fought over who was going to get the comics first in the American newspapers, especially on Sundays. Back then famous national cartoon characters such as Dick Tracy, Terry and the Pirates, Blondie and Dagwood Bumstead, and a whole host of others excited us and held our interest. It was these popular cultural cartoon icons that intrigued me early on and ultimately inspired me to learn to read and write.

I first acquired these skills, not in nursery school or even in kindergarten, but in my mother's kitchen. We lived in a five-room railroad flat in a tenement located in Manhattan's Spanish Harlem. This severely limited space housed ten people. I was an active, curious four-year-old with six older brothers who were all in school. In such a restricted area my mother had to find ways in which to proceed with her daily routine of running a clean, orderly household and keeping me safely occupied. Her futile efforts to teach me embroidery caused me to have such terrible tantrums that she finally gave up trying to amuse me with the art of needle and thread. After countless spankings and rebukes for all of my mischief-making games that resulted in broken pieces of her best crystal and making tatters out of her handmade lace tablecloth, my mother was at her wit's end. "At four-and-a-half years old, you're as bad as my sons or worse," she'd scold, "just a tomboy!" Finally I was relegated to help with cleaning and cooking chores alongside my mother so that she could keep a sharp eye on me.

Unbearably bored, I made several attempts to read the comics in the daily newspaper and figure out the story, but I had no success. Then one day I approached my mother and asked her to explain who these cartoon characters were. I pointed to the words in the balloons over their heads and demanded, "What are they saying?" Quickly my mother found some scrap paper and a pencil and set me up at the kitchen table. With care and deliberation, she demonstrated how to copy the cartoon characters. My mother's sketch of Dick Tracy looked pretty good to me. To my surprise my first drawing wasn't half bad. "That's very good" was my mother's reaction. Her support inspired me. I went on to do some more drawings. "Wonderful! What a smart daughter I have!"

I can still vividly recall that feeling of elation the moment I knew without a doubt that I could actually read all by myself!

High praise from my mother made me very determined to impress her even more. That meant I *had* to succeed. As I continued my drawings improved. Although nothing could have made me happier than having my mother's approval, I still remained curious about those words in the balloons. But my repeated inquiries seemed to slide by my mother, who appeared to ignore my questions. Even at this early age and without understanding the circumstances,

I somehow understood that my mother didn't know what those words meant. The reality was that my mother could not read or write in English. She had the equivalent of a fourth-grade education and, even in her native language of Spanish, had limited reading and writing skills.

Almost overnight, reading gave me a sense of freedom. My excitement was overwhelming when I discovered the power of words.

It was with the sweet sounds of Puerto Rican Spanish that my mother first spoke to me and sang her songs. I always communicated in Spanish with my mother and the other adults in my household, my father and aunt. However, my brothers and I spoke mostly in English among ourselves. Therefore, to a large extent, I grew up bilingual.

As much as I enjoyed drawing, I still yearned to know what those comic-strip characters were saying. My younger brothers became impatient with my questions and dismissed my curiosity, so I approached my oldest brother Vincent. He was the serious one, the scholar who maintained a straight-A average and expressed a thirst for knowledge. Patiently he set out to teach me how to read. He would print the letters of the alphabet and insist that I copy each one over for as many times as necessary until he was convinced I had gotten it correctly. He explained that all words are comprised of only twenty-six letters. Once I learned my alphabet, Vincent guaranteed that I too would be able to read and write.

Each day I had to choose one word from inside the white balloons over a comic-strip character. For example, if the word spelled "running," Vincent would instruct me to select the correct characters from the alphabet and print them in proper order on a separate slip of paper. Then I was to re-print the word several times in my notebook. I was an eager and willing student and worked hard on my lessons. Quite soon I was able to pick whole phrases from the comics and understand what they said. I can still vividly recall that feeling of elation the moment I knew without a doubt that I could actually read all by myself!

Almost overnight, reading gave me a sense of freedom. My excitement was overwhelming when I discovered the power of words. I went wild with excitement as I read labels on food products, wanting to know what some of the complicated words on the food labels meant. I'd ask my brother Vincent to define what "homogenized" on a milk carton was all about and what exactly did the word "sodium" or the phrase "puree of tomato" mean. More often than not, my brother was patient enough to find these words in the dictionary and read their meaning aloud to me. We did not have encyclopedias at home, but it was only a few years later in the public library that I was able to find out in detail the meaning and history of words and phrases. But at that time, during the infancy of my reading abilities, it was all quite awesome. Furthermore, I could help explain the headlines in the English language newspapers to my mother and that made me feel very important indeed.

So, perhaps because there was no television back then and my mother could find nothing else to amuse me, I began my love affair with reading. Life presented exciting challenges and great possibilities, and I was ready to greet those expectations with enthusiasm.

I was a child who did not fit into the stereotype of the so-called "average" American girl.

My day to go to Kindergarten (a word I already knew how to spell), my very first day of school, was to be a bitter disappointment. I had been warned to "be a good girl and do exactly as you are told." With happy anticipation I sat at my desk watching my teacher with a sense of awe. What mysteries would teacher reveal and what new worlds of wonder was I about to discover? I was so eager that when my teacher asked the first question I shot up my hand, desperate to show her all that I had learned. She asked that I count to ten. I stood and counted beyond ten, for I could count as high as 100! Teacher interrupted me and told me to come to the front of the class, then warned that I was not to take it upon myself to speak out of turn or offer information that had not been requested. I still can feel the humiliation as she dug her index finger into the middle of my shoulder blades before she sent me back to my seat.

Even though most of us had been born in the United States, or had arrived when we were infants or toddlers, many of my classmates were Hispanics, mostly of Puerto Rican origin. Often we spoke among ourselves in Spanish or in Spanglish. This made teacher furious and she'd declare, ". . . [W]e speak English in the United States of America," reminding us that we were not in our old country and warning us never to speak Spanish in class. Repeatedly, she questioned our loyalty and gratitude to America, thereby labeling us as ingrates or, at best, second-class citizens. Once when a little girl did not understand the teacher, I forgot my resolution to stay passive and took it upon myself to translate what was said into Spanish. Before my classmate could respond, teacher's anger exploded and she labeled me the "class showoff." Thereafter, I was addressed by this new label more often than by my given name. She warned that if everyone acted like me, no one would do any better than their parents; we would all be destined for failure. "Where, where indeed," she demanded, "was our gratitude and loyalty to America?" Of course, she had never sat down and had a real conversation with my parents, my wonderfully bright and compassionate mother or my hard-working honorable father. In fact, I suspect she hadn't gotten to know any of the parents of the children, yet she felt no compunction about judging our families in a harsh and demeaning manner. We all listened obediently and no one dared to respond.

After that incident, I was often made an example of by being sent to sit facing the "wall." I remember the "wall"; it was bare and painted pea green. It was lonely and, although I was being punished, I'd use this opportunity to create another ambience. I would fantasize by squinting my eyes. While searching for discoloration in the paint, a crack in the plaster or shadows on the surface, I'd visualize trees, a waterfall and, in one spot, I imagined the profile of a horse. My humiliation, my embarrassment and anger at teacher was ameliorated by this game that somehow helped ease my punishment. I now recognize that it also sharpened my sense of imagination and provided yet another survival skill to be used under oppressive circumstances. However, in the end, teacher was the adult, the one with the power, and I withdrew by sitting quietly and suppressing my desire to be seen and heard. Fortunately I had already achieved the ability to gather knowledge, and it proved to be more powerful than teacher's rejection. That achievement granted me the self-esteem to overcome the nonacceptance and contempt that had contaminated my introduction to our public school system.

Another significant turn of events happened when I was seven and my brother Vincent took me to the library. Library card in hand, I took out my first book, Collodi's *Pinocchio*. I thought I would never again read such a wonderful book. But the librarians showed me other books about history, adventure, fiction, and poetry. The library was my home away from home. In their reading room, I began to put reading skills and creative thinking abilities to practical use. I found books that allowed me to challenge, investigate, and learn.

For example, I was able to look at the World Atlas and discover the difference between countries and continents and locate the United States, Europe, and Asia. I was amazed when I realized that Egypt was in Africa! And, I remember being excited when I found the small island of Puerto Rico in the Greater Antilles. A librarian introduced me to the books of Howard Fast. I read many of his titles including *Citizen Tom Paine* (1943), and *Patrick Henry and the Frigate's Keel, and Other Stories of a Young Nation* (1945), and began to understand and enjoy American History. I loved the works of Jack London and read *Call of the Wild* (1903), several times. Later on early in high school I discovered the writing of Richard Wright. Published literature about Blacks by Blacks was rare and I still remember how profoundly his novel *Native Son* (1940) affected me. I continued to read, and I went on to appreciate the Greek classics, Shakespeare, George Bernard Shaw, and all the great Russian novelists; in fact reading allowed my imagination to soar. However, my greatest pleasure came from browsing through the encyclopedias which provided me with the freedom to explore. I was able to use these books in order to investigate and put the required information into my school reports. Learning became fun! My first loves, however, were drawing and painting and, as a senior in high school, a brand new world opened up for me when I discovered art books. However, it was when I saw the work of the Mexican artists and mural painters, such as Frieda Kahlo, Diego Rivera, and Jose Clemente Orozco, for the first time that I considered that perhaps one day I too could create art in a serious way; success became a real possibility.

But while I was still learning to use my reading skills back in second grade, I experienced my first independent activity. It happened when, just like my older siblings, I participated in our national American pastime and sent off the required money with the boxtop of a popular breakfast cereal. I waited with happy anticipation for that special magic ring or a set of super, three-dimensional spy glasses. When the package arrived, the treasures were never as exciting or as neat as I had imagined. But I continued to send off boxtops because being a member of this famous national "cereal" club amended such disappointments.

So perhaps because there was no television back then and my mother could find nothing else to amuse me, I began my love affair with reading.

I continued my visits to the library, reading voraciously. However, when I searched for books that represented me and my family, I did not find them. I never saw myself, my family, our customs, or our contribution to our nation in any book, anywhere. My family and I did not exist in the world of children's literature. Now as I think back I shudder to imagine where I might be today had I not learned to read before I got into public school.

Exclusion is an endemic part of our greater society-at-large, as evidenced by the lack of and/or limited representation of American Indians, African Americans, and Hispanic Americans in mainstream publishing, television, government, and so on. It is no mystery to me that the negative consequences of this disparity filters down and corrupts our educational system. This corruption results in shutting out those who do not appear to fit the stereotype of the all White, all-American, well-adjusted middle-class child.

In school I was told it was wrong to embrace my Puerto Rican background because I would be viewed as disloyal to my country, as an ungrateful American. Yet, early on I recognized that the Latinos stereotyped in films and on television, such as the "Frito Bandito's", "Carmen Miranda's," and "Anita's and Maria's" of "West Side Story," had little to do with me, my parents or the folks I admired in my community. In my heart I knew that honoring the courage of my mother and parents who had emigrated to a foreign and hostile environment in order to give their children a better life was imperative. I also recognized that I was not being welcomed into the greater society-at-large where there seemed to be no available role or place for me. My being Puerto Rican, however, provided me a sense of identity, dignity, and purpose. I was somebody in my own community where, no matter how tough or poor my environment might be, I was not perceived as a stranger or an unwanted intruder.

It is dangerous when an important segment of our children see people like themselves represented in such a negative manner on the nightly TV news, or in films and magazines, and never or rarely see themselves reflected in our educational curriculum or in our literature. Many of these young people will grow up convinced that they don't have a right to be involved in this nation's future and that their input will make no difference.

I see this as a serious problem when I am lecturing in public schools, from grammar all the way up to high school, where the majority of students are Latino. Except for leaders in their immediate communities, these students have never been given the opportunity to identify with strong and positive role models outside of their neighborhoods. Latino figures who have national or international notoriety in sports and show business are beyond reach and far from their everyday reality. Consequently, these young people are dumbstruck to meet a successful Latina. When I relate my personal background and share my experiences of growing up female and Puerto Rican, students are absolutely incredulous that I am a real live person. When I ask young people to tell me about famous and accomplished Latinos in the fields of literature, the arts, science, or government, I am dismayed at their answers. They know little or nothing about the many other accomplished Latinos who have excelled in education, government, medicine, and just about every imaginable discipline. Surely this information in the form of books, films, audio and video cassettes is available and could easily be included in their school curriculum. These students carry tremendous obstacles to learning, because of their lack of self-esteem and feelings of exclusion and rejection. It is no wonder that only a small percentage are able to go on to higher education.

Yet, when I lecture to Caucasian students, they clearly display a sincere fascination with other ethnic American cultures. I see keen curiosity in their eyes and real interest in their questions. These White and middle-class students have read my books and identified with all of the human attributes of my heroes, such as Felita. They connect with her warm relationship with her *abuelita*, her grandmother, her mishaps, and especially her quarrel with her very best friend and how they make up. Very popular, too, is Felita's first innocent romantic kiss. Above and beyond these human experiences, they also want to know more about Latino culture. What about the barrio . . . neighborhood? How are these Spanish names and words pronounced? What kind of food is eaten? How do they celebrate our national holidays? How wonderful that they remain curious and hungry for knowledge, that they want to learn about other cultures that make up these United States.

The library was my home away from home. . . .
I found books that allowed me to challenge,
investigate, and learn.

However, one of the most striking differences that I have observed between our Caucasian students and students of color comes from an answer to my question, "What are you . . . what is your background?" Almost always Caucasian students answer, "I'm nothing" or "I don't know." It is true that my question is not specific; for example, I do not ask "What is your religion or race or ethnicity?" or "Do you consider yourself connected to your state or national region, that is, do you see yourself as a Southerner, Midwesterner, Easterner, or the like?" Although these Caucasian students' ancestors have been in America for several generations, they do not seem to fully comprehend the meaning of that question. In fact, they have never, not once, asked me to clarify my question. How then do they define themselves as Americans within these United States?

On the other hand, students of color and/or of immigrant parents answer with a certain amount of pride, "I'm Latino, Hispanic American, Asian American, Jewish, Black, or Native American." These students have a strong identity with their cultural background, whereas White children do not seem to fully comprehend the meaning of that question. Is race or ethnicity then, within our nation, the most distinguishing feature of determining the kind of American one is?

In school, I was told it was wrong to embrace my Puerto Rican background because I would be viewed as disloyal to my country, as an ungrateful American.

Our nation is unique compared to any other country on this planet because of our diverse ethnic population. How this heterogeneousness is incorporated into our society has a strong impact on our young people. Understanding who is an American, outside of the Eurocentric stereotype, demands a certain amount of imagination and courage on the part of our education system. It calls for a recognition and appreciation of *all* of our children by a guarantee that they be represented accurately and included in our public school curriculum in all fifty states.

It will unite and reinforce our nation when American children of any race or ethnic background can collectively feel pride in the courageous history of Native Americans and African Americans. The curriculum of our schools should deal with themes that cover our entire history, including the elimination of many American Indian nations and the consequences of the slave industry. Students should be taught that Hispanics have contributed much to the founding of these United States and that California and most of the West were once Spanish territories where everyone spoke Spanish. History should acknowledge the great numbers of Chinese who risked their lives in the building of the railroads across this nation. All our students should be educated about the American internment camps that held Japanese Americans during World War II, a shameful lesson of racism never to be repeated again.

Our educators and administrators must provide our children with a foundation of knowledge that will allow them to appreciate a complete representation of our indigenous population. This basis should necessarily include the input of those peoples who, at the outset, arrived from all corners of the earth and who have been responsible for the building and preservation of these United States. It is long overdue that, alongside George Washington, Thomas Jefferson, Benjamin Franklin, the Pilgrims and the *Mayflower*, *all* of our children and their ancestors be recognized for their place in American history.

It is impossible to be proud of who you are if you don't know your own history. The making of these United States was accomplished by many different kinds of people and unless they share an equal place in history, our books and curriculum will remain exclusionary and incomplete. As the children of new immigrants fill our schools, they should know that people of color have also helped to build this nation. Being an American is different from any other nationality in the world because it includes people from all over the globe and that reality should be taught as a source of pride to our children.

I do not want to end this article without acknowledging the many determined and valiant educators who fight the good battle to provide all of our children with a good and equitable education. One example is the ongoing attempt to save bilingual education. Those courageous educators and teachers who fight to keep bilingual programs from going under must not only be praised and appreciated, but supported. After all, in the finest and most expensive private schools, students are tutored and encouraged to become proficient in a second language. Such irony seems lost when it comes to educating our most precious resource, our children.

Finally, I would like to impress upon you that I am a perfect example of what the FREEDOM TO READ can produce, and I imagine that is why I still remain an optimist. For it is my belief that, when all of our children are represented in the preparation of our school curriculum, we will open up the door to a whole new generation whose originality and energy could well make our nation the most powerful and innovative place on the face of this earth.

When I am asked, "How come you learned to read and write and became successful? And, why can't others take advantage of our school system and do as you did?" I respond that if I had I not had the desire to learn and been given the skills of reading *before* I got into our public school system, that question might well be irrelevant.

References

Fast, H. (1943). *Citizen Tom Paine*. New York: Duell, Sloan and Pearce.

Fast, H. (1945). *Patrick Henry and the frigate's keel, and other stories of a young nation*. New York: Duell, Sloan and Pearce.

London, J. (1903). *The call of the wild*. New York: Macmillan.

Wright, R. (1940). *Native son*. New York: Harper and Brothers.

Books by Nicholasa Mohr

Mohr, N. (1979). *Felita*. Ill. Ray Cruz. New York: Bantam Doubleday.

Mohr, N. (1985). *Rituals of survival: A woman's portfolio*. Houston: Arte Publico Press.

Mohr, N. (1986). *Going home*. New York: Bantam Skylark.

Mohr, N. (1986). *Nilda*. Houston: Arte Publico Press.

Mohr, N. (1988). *In Nueva York*. New York: Arte Publico Press.

Mohr, N. (1993). *El Bronx remembered*. New York: Harper Trophy Book.

Mohr, N. (1994). *Growing up inside the sanctuary of my imagination*. New York: Simon & Schuster.

Mohr, N. (1995). *The magic shell*. Ill. Rudy Gutierrez. New York: Scholastic.

Mohr, N. (1995). *El regalo mágico*. Ill. Rudy Gutierrez. New York: Scholastic.

Mohr, N. & Martorell, A. (1995). *The song of el coquí and other tales of Puerto Rico*. New York: Viking.

Mohr, N. (1995). *La canción del coquí y otros cuentos de Puerto Rico*. New York: Viking.

Mohr, N. (1996). *Old Letivia and the Mountain of Sorrows*. Ill. Rudy Gutierrez. New York: Viking.

Mohr, N. (1996). *La vieja Letivia y el Monte de los Pesares*. Ill. Rudy Gutierrez. New York: Viking.

Mohr, N. (1997). *A matter of pride and other stories*. Houston: Arte Publico Press.

Conferring with Struggling Readers:
The Test of Our Craft, Courage, and Hope

Randy Bomer

Malika, a peanut of a girl with incongruously chubby cheeks and giant glasses, looks back down at her book, but only because I gesture toward it and lift it a little toward her eyes. She can think of several other things she would like to talk about instead of keeping up the hard work of reading. Sighing, she starts the next sentence, "He went down the road," pressing out each phoneme, one at a time. "Hhh-ee-ww-eh-nn-tuh-duh-ow-nn-th-uh-" and she freezes at "road."

After a long pause, I say gently, "What did he go down, Malika? What's he doing?" pointing to the picture of a man walking down a road. Even as I do so, I know there are still ways for her to get confused. A still picture, even a close illustration of textual content, cannot really convey the movement in the phrase, "down the road." Malika, frozen in her tracks, certainly has no feeling of motion, no ongoing sense of moving down the road.

"He's walking," she says, uneasily looking up. I had of course hoped she would keep looking at the text, focusing on what she was trying to figure out, while maintaining the sense of what was happening.

"Yeah, and let's look. Where's he walking?"

She points to a house on the page, farther down the road. I wish she had said "down the road," and so solved the mystery meaningfully, but I just say, "OK, let's see. Where'd he go?" I point to the beginning of the same sentence. She returns to her emphatic sounding of each letter until she gets to "road" and pauses again. I wait, and finally she slowly enunciates "rrr-oh-duh." She looks up. "I don't know."

"You don't know what?"

"I don't know what it says!"

Randy Bomer is an Assistant Professor of Education at Queens College, City University of New York. He is author of *Time for Meaning* (Heinemann, 1995).

"But you just *said* it, Malika. Read the sentence again, and really listen and think about what you're saying. Read it to your own mind."

She does it all again, and again she says, "I don't know."

"Let me say back for you what you just said, and see if it makes sense. 'He went down the road.'"

"Oh!" She slaps her forehead with both hands. "I'm so stupid! Stupid! Stupid!"

Naturally, I say she's not stupid and point out all that she is managing to do. She probably knew I would say that; it's all part of the dance.

Working with students like Malika, I think again about the human reality of words I use lightly, "struggling reader." I think of the serious meaning of the word "struggle," like wrestling a sumo, like trudging over the Himalayas, like class struggle. The word implies weight, a great expense of effort against resistance over time. For Malika, this struggle has gone on every weekday for several years. I can think of nothing at which I have had to work so hard, cannot remember ever feeling so poor while striving for so long. I feel awe at the difficulty endured by struggling readers, a respect for their effort and even their despair.

I do not mean to present Malika as a "typical" struggling reader, because I do not believe that such a person exists. There is no such thing as *The Struggling Reader*—since all who struggle do so in intricately unique ways, experiencing different snarls of confusion, peculiar exertions, idiosyncratic theories of literacy, and unusual habits of mind. These individual characteristics are not biological defects or intellectual deficiencies, but rather are the outcome of a particular person meeting special conditions, for example, instructional practices (Coles, 1987; Edwards & Mercer, 1987; Holt, 1969; McDermott & Gospodinoff, 1975; Mehan, 1982; Rose, 1989; Taylor, 1991). The expectations of school make "struggling reader" a category in our minds as teachers. That does not, however, mean that these students all "lack" the same things or that they all need the same kinds of support. No pill exists to cure what ails them, and whenever anyone offers a sure and easy remedy, we should suspect simplemindedness or fraud. Like other aspects of teaching, supporting struggling readers requires inquiry, reflectiveness, and depth of understanding. Unfortunately, there is a tendency in schools to make the teaching of vulnerable readers more heavily scripted and mechanistic. Such a response denies the deepest resources of meaning, thoughtfulness, and respect to the students who need them most (Allington, 1980; Rhodes & Dudley-Marling, 1996; Smith, 1984; Walmsley & Allington, 1995).

Examining Reading Conferences in Upper Grade Classrooms

For a year, I learned about struggling readers with a group of classroom teachers, reading teachers, and staff developers at the Teachers College Reading Project. We worked together with students, separately conducted case studies, met monthly to analyze data, and worked to clarify our practice with struggling readers. We inquired into both policy and practice. This article focuses on our work with reading conferences during upper grade independent reading workshops.

When I say "independent reading workshop," I refer to a time in the school day, almost every day, usually a half-hour to an hour in duration, when students read books they have chosen. They choose books from the classroom library, primarily, but also from the school library, home, public libraries, and friends. The teacher may present a short mini-lesson at the beginning of the workshop, and there may be a whole-class reflective meeting at the end. During the bulk of the time, students read, and the teacher mostly confers with individuals, assessing, assigning individual strategies, and providing support at all levels of the reading process. Most teachers in our group felt challenged to tip their attention at least somewhat in favor of the students who needed the most support, though not to the extent that such a decision cost the rest of the students too dearly.

We focused much of our work on the independent reading workshop for several reasons. First, we reasoned that we had to confer with readers during that time anyway, and the struggling readers tended to present us—and other teachers we knew—with seriously confusing moments. Second, we saw independent reading as the bottom line in reading instruction; everything else we did had to support students' own reading lives. We thought it wisest to concentrate our attention on what was most essential in reading, students' ways of working with texts when teachers weren't around. Third, when students read books they have chosen, they have already activated some knowledge (in order even to select the book); they have mentally engaged with what they predict will be in the text and have attached their intentions and purposes to it.

I will discuss the need to work carefully with students to help them choose wisely, but when they *do* choose their own books well, the need for elaborate teacher-designed pre-reading procedures and book orientations is obviated. Those motivational, schemata-activating, preliminary engagements that occupy much space in the literature on teaching struggling readers are designed, we thought, to undo the damage done to reading by the authoritative structure of schooling and the sometimes (but not always) necessary reality of teachers selecting reading material for students. Intentional, independent reading seemed a classroom structure that allowed us to approach the reading processes of our students most directly.

We chose the classrooms in which we worked also because of the strong social life that surrounded reading in them. In these classes, the teacher and children successfully constructed a shared understanding of what reading was all about, a lived philosophy about things such as: why reading is important, the kinds of thinking it helps make possible, and the ways readers can think together. Students had daily opportunities to talk with their teacher and each other about their reading processes and habits, to discuss the ideas they built with texts they read together and separately, and to share books as central reference points in classroom life. Though the exact structures employed in classrooms varied, students participated in partnerships (two students together for either a short or long time), reading centers (fairly short-term groupings of students with multiple texts around a shared topic), reading clubs (long-term, self-selected groups of students who read a number of books together over time), chat groups (thematically-based groups wherein different students were reading different books, meeting only once or a few times), and whole-class shared texts (read-alouds as well as times when everyone had a copy and read separately, coming together for discussions). In any given school year, a student moved through several of these social arrangements and, in each of them, the reading demands were different. We believed that such variety in experience strengthened readers and made their thinking-with-books more flexible by shifting the social context of their cognition (Cole, 1996; Lave & Wenger, 1991). In other words, it was important to us that students' thinking be mediated by diverse kinds of activity in diverse social arrangements (Vygotsky, 1962; Wertsch, 1991).

The expectations of school make "struggling reader" a category in our minds as teachers. That does not, however, mean that these students all "lack" the same things or that they need the same kinds of support.

Because we saw reading and learning to read as social, these arrangements were crucial considerations for us, but they were problematic as well. The students from whom we wanted to learn could only benefit partially from the social interactions we thought were so important. For example, if the conversation in a reading club was mostly about how the character in the present book compared to one in a book the group had previously read, then a struggling reader could participate as a member of the group, even if she had to infer much from the talk and fudge the details. *But* this conversation would not help her enough in the foundational work of making meaning with print on the run while reading. Reading growth proceeds along multiple lines, and there is not a single zone of proximal development. Conversations that help a reader develop on one front may leave work yet to be done in other zones. This conversation would be useful, to be sure, in its enrichment of the semantic cuing system (Goodman, 1967; Goodman & Burke, 1980), but the conversation is exercising thinking that could be a response to a movie. The reader is not at that moment working on the closer-in work of reading, thinking in collaboration with print. In order to support the cognition guided and constrained by the visual words of a text, the reader needs another kind of conversation. The work is still social, since the struggling reader needs his thinking to be externalized, distributed, "scaffolded," in Bruner's terminology (Wood, Bruner, & Ross, 1976), but since it is so closely tied to texts, it requires a smaller social unit, more of a partnership. Since most of the children in these classes did not need to grow through this same kind of relatively telescopic attention to text, it was most pedagogically practical for the teacher and other support people to play the role of the partner, and it was the nature of this role that we were trying to explore. Therefore, even though these were conferences with individual students, the experience of reading and the process of learning were still located in social contexts. Furthermore, it is important to keep in mind that the conferences I will describe are only a few of the social engagements in which these readers participated. Struggling readers need *both* rich conversations about big ideas in texts, which let them participate as full members of a literate community, *and* interactions that support figuring out the details of the textual world.

We tried to keep in mind, when conferring with struggling readers, that we needed to approach them with humility, with tact (Van Manen, 1991), remembering that, though we might know more about how their reading *should* go, we knew much less than they about how their reading *was* going. They were the experts on the vagaries of their own attention, on the knowledge they used to figure out meaning with print, and on the ways they marshaled their energy and desire to understand. We respected the mystery of the nature of reading in their minds even as we worked in direct, close ways to reformulate their processes. We noted that, often before, these students had been approached in a brisk, intrusive instructional manner, where the teacher had absolutely certain knowledge of what the text said and where the inquiring process of figuring-out was shut down before it began. We reined ourselves in, forced ourselves to relax, and played the role of partner in exploration.

Teaching Readers to Choose Books Wisely

In a New York City classroom, I observe J.T., a twelve-year-old who is still in fifth grade. J.T. looks older than the other boys in his class, partly because he is taller and partly because he wears such cool clothes, like a gangsta rapper. He has on baggy jeans he is constantly told to pull up, a hooded NFL sweat top, and a knit cap pulled low over his eyebrows. When he looks at you, it is through the bottom fibers of this cap. Obviously, he presents himself for effect.

Two days ago, he chose *My Darling, My Hamburger* by Paul Zindel (1984) from the classroom library after abandoning *My Side of the Mountain* (George, 1959). Today, he opens the book to what seems a random page and frowns at it for about twenty seconds. Then he looks up absently and flips the pages of the book, feeling them rub across his thumb. He fans his face with the pages this way, then stretches his long arm toward John and waves the book in John's face. John scowls and humps his back at J.T., who then gets up, walks to another seat, opens the book again, and looks at a page for a little while.

For struggling readers in upper grade classrooms, the business of choosing books is complex. First of all, the child has a felt need to look, to his peers, as mature as anyone else in the community. Since difficulty of text is one of the clearest symbols of development in elementary and middle school, he has a reasonable desire to be seen carrying an adult-looking text. In J.T.'s case, the book was part of the costume, little more. His behavior, as I stood back and watched, suggested he was not, to say the least, deeply engaged with his novel. Struggling readers are so used to having reading feel like nonsense that it probably made little difference to him which book he held in his hands.

I asked J.T. if I could talk to him and took him to a relatively under-populated corner of the crowded classroom. I asked him to open the book to the page he was on, and he flipped thoughtfully to page 83.

"So this is where you've gotten to?" I asked. "J.T., if I were to ask you to tell me what's going on at this point in the book, would you feel nervous or sure of yourself or what?"

"Oh, wait," he said, scowling, and he flipped back to page 44, apparently thinking I was just questioning his account of his progress. I said that was fine, and then I asked him the same question again.

"Um . . . well, I might be kind of nervous," he said, "because this book, it's weird."

"Yeah, maybe it is kind of weird," I said. "But let's talk about something. You know how it is when you're talking to somebody, and you know exactly what they're saying? That feeling of *understanding?* In your mind, it makes sense, and you're going, yeah . . . yeah. . . . Or if you watch something on TV, right from the beginning, and you know the show, and you're right with it? So that's understanding. And you also know the feeling when someone's talking to you, and you have no idea what they're talking about? Or you come in on some movie on TV, and you're like, 'What's going on?' That's *confusion.* There's understanding and confusion, and reading should almost always feel like understanding. So, with that in mind, let's go back to the start of this book, and you read to yourself the first couple of pages."

J.T. read, and I skimmed over his shoulder, in case we ended up discussing it. After a few minutes, he looked up and said, "Confusion," and sort of laughed.

I asked him if the books that usually feel like understanding to him *look* like this book or if they look different. He said that usually the words (the print) were bigger.

I took him over to the classroom library and pulled down five books that varied in difficulty. Arraying the books in front of him, I asked him to rank them, left to right, from books that felt like understanding to books that felt like confusion. I assured him he wouldn't have to choose any of those books to read if he didn't want to. All we were doing for now was identifying his kind of book at this point in his reading life. When we'd finished, I said, he'd be able to choose a book of the same kind that looked interesting to him. While he worked on ranking the books, I had quick conferences with a couple of other kids.

If students are to grow as readers, they have to work with texts that are meaningful to them. Interest and intention were fundamental values to members of our study group in conducting independent reading workshops, but we realized that could not mean any book that "looked good" to a student was an appropriate tool for his growth. In supporting student choice, we found it necessary to teach readers to choose wisely. In the past, we had corrected students' choices decisively, as Atwell (1986) describes herself doing, or we had, too often, just let it go, believing that maybe the reader would derive something from the experience. Now, because we knew that learning to read would require more time with print than we could oversee, because we wanted to teach habits that would make reading self-sustaining in the life of the reader, we needed to address the student as a responsible decision-maker.

Effective readers continually monitor for sense, checking to make sure they are experiencing understanding as they move through text. When I am reading in bed before I go to sleep and I suddenly realize that the last page and a half of print has not affected my thought at all, I notice, and turn out the light. Struggling readers don't notice—to them, everything seems fine, because that barrenness of meaning is what they're used to. They do know, however, what understanding feels like in lots of other situations, especially ones that do not involve print. And it's that feeling that needs to be reawakened in them when choosing books. I want them to expect understanding, to hunger for it and, when it is absent, to put the book down and get away from it. Sure, once they are reading a book that's right for them, we can work on some strategies for figuring out confusing parts. But such work is only useful within a general context of sense-making.

There is a tendency in schools to make the teaching of vulnerable readers more heavily scripted and mechanistic. Such a response denies the deepest resources of meaning, thoughtfulness, and respect to the students who need them the most.

When I came back to J.T., he had ranked the books in order of his experience of understanding. If a fixed scale of difficulty existed, I would say he had gotten the order wrong once or twice. Since the task was for him to attend to his own feeling of clarity or confusion, however, and since more is involved in reading difficulty than is hinted at in readability formulae, I trusted he was right. I asked him to pick the book that gave him the strongest feeling of understanding. He selected one, and I gathered up the others and put them back on the shelves.

"OK," I said, "that's going to be your example, your model, for the *kind* of books you need to pick. Whenever you go to the shelves here or at the library, at least for the next few weeks, have that with you. The ones you choose should probably look kind of like that one, and they definitely should feel like that one—like understanding. But you may not be that interested in the topic for your model book. The others you choose should have a lot of interest for you, so they give you a lot of energy to read."

Looking from J.T.'s hooded face to the book in his hands, though, I was apprehensive. It was an "early" chapter book, easier than, say, Pee-Wee Scouts books, but with similarly cartoonish pictures of young children. Looking from the book to the boy, I worried about how long he would stick with this project of growing into reading. I knew there were less-embarrassing-looking but easy-to-read books available in his school, and that he would probably find them. However, those had been around before, and there was a reason he had not chosen them. I wanted him to turn an important corner in his reading development: to begin choosing books that would help him be strong as a reader rather than going on being an impostor, constantly aware of his failures. He and I both needed to face reality and tell the truth.

Becoming minimally competent is not especially motivating. Without these larger, more meaningful pursuits as part of a life with reading, why bother getting better at it?

I looked at him and tried to assume a serious tone of eye-to-eye talk. "Reading has to make sense, J.T. You need to feel strong and smart. When you read those other books, you feel weak and small—so stay away from those for now. You *will* be able to read them, if you do what you need to and get stronger. You want your arms to be strong, you do it one curl at a time, with the weight you can lift. You don't get strong by trying to pick up a car. To get strong as a reader, you do it one book at a time, and you work with the books you can read, the ones where you feel understanding."

Still looking at the book he was holding, I realized this was not going to take him long to read. I remembered his goofing off earlier in the workshop and wanted to find a way to keep him working. I asked him, when he took his model book back to the shelves, to pick not just one book, but a little stack of books that he would like to try. I gave him a plastic bag with a zipper to keep them in. This stack would become his book collection, and he could have those with him during reading periods. He should read those as many times as he wanted to, and I encouraged him to read them more than once. When he was ready, he could trade one or two of them for new books to replace them.

A few days later, I checked in with J. T. again. In his book collection, he had several nonfiction books he'd gathered from classrooms up and down the hall where his class was located. The books he had chosen were mostly about sports, insects, and animals, and they had more of a magazine-like appearance, with photo-illustrations rather than the cartoonish drawing. (I regret not writing down the titles because I can't share them with you here. There was nothing magical about them, though, and the same type of book is not hard to find: the thinnest books in the sports and science shelves of the children's section of any large book store.) I could see immediately the advantage of these books over his initial choice; there was less potential for shame.

Our inquiry group found this kind of conference useful over and over, focusing on the reader's experience of understanding, choosing a template book, and using that book to choose a mini-library. These stacks of books, like the piles my friends all have on their nightstands, the ones they mean to get to soon, became for us and our students a vision of possibility, a promise of new worlds.

Running Alongside Readers in Conferences

Though we wanted students to be able to make decisions that supported their independent reading, our group thought that, after the students were reading more appropriate books, the teacher could not exit the scene. Having kids work with text they could read was, to us, necessary but not sufficient for reading growth. We still believed students needed to be coached in the act of reading, so we developed our conferences as assisted performance (Tharp & Gallimore, 1988; Vygotsky, 1962) in *thinking* about the world of the text while figuring out print. Most of the time in these conferences, we tried to be representatives of meaning in the story, reminding the reader that what they said (i.e., read aloud) should make sense in the whole of the text.

When we thought it was the most important thing to teach, we also directed the reader's attention to letters and their sounds. For many of the struggling readers with whom we worked, observations of their writing behaviors and the texts they produced showed us that they knew at least one written way to represent the sounds they spoke. Sometimes, they did not draw on that knowledge when they read, however, and we reminded them, "you just wrote that sound today," or, "that one's in Jerry's name, remember?" Other times, a text presented them with an unfamiliar way of representing a sound (for example, "gh" where they might have written "f") and, at those times, we focused their attention on that spelling and showed other examples before going on with the story.

Other times, when a reader had trouble with a high-frequency word that was difficult to predict from meaning (for example, "because" or "always"), we asked the reader if we could just "pause" the story for a couple of minutes, and we lifted the word from the context, writing it on a slip of paper the reader could use as a bookmark, and discussing with the child its meaning, its parts, its sounds, and its physical shape on the page. On these slips of paper (sometimes they were sticky notes), we would sometimes accumulate, across several conferences, four or five words, with the reader adding her own whenever she wanted to. More than a small number of words, we thought, would result in diminishing returns, as it does in spelling (Wilde, 1992).

As we had done in writing conferences, we stayed with the reader just long enough to teach one or two things about reading that could apply not only to the present text but also to future reading. Our purpose in the conference was to help the reader construct durable understanding about a bit of the reading process, not merely to get her through this text today. Like running alongside someone learning to ride a bicycle (Tharp & Gallimore, 1988), we read along with struggling readers, whispering cues, for example, to look at the first letter, to check what they said/read against the way we usually say things, to monitor whether what they were saying fit with their sense of how the world goes, to guess about what was coming based on their evolving understanding of the text-world. This running alongside was quick and often confusing work, and we often found it hard to make split-second decisions about just what to say to a reader at a particular second while also staying relaxed, easy, supportive, and inquiring. For a while, it helped us to carry a cheat-sheet of guidelines:

Figuring Out What It Says—Guidelines for Read-Along Conferences

- Speak softly, gently. Think of yourself as a voice inside the reader's head—because you will be.
- Interview first to find out what the reader is thinking and doing with this book. Find out how he is participating in the world of this book and how he is expecting it to go on from here.
- Aim through the reading for meaning. Act as if the child is telling you something that's supposed to make sense, rather than acting as if the student is performing "reading." Say, "What'd you say???" or "He did what???" as you would to yourself if you read something that didn't make sense to you.
- If the reader stops, wait. After singing something silently to yourself, ask what she is thinking.
- One thing to ask is, "What would make sense?" or "What *could* that be?" This asks the reader to make a guess based on sense-making.
- If the reader seems inattentive to print, ask "Does that look right?" This cues the reader to see if the letters, based on the sounds they make, could say the word they guessed from meaning. Then move on and get back to the story.
- If the reader guesses something that does not fit in the sentence grammatically, you can say, "Does that sound right?" or "Is that how we say it?" If it sounds OK to the reader, move on, and get back to the story.
- Sometimes, take this as an opportunity to talk about strategies for figuring out what it says, such as:
  - reaching for more of the sentence, then trying the word again,
  - going back to the start of the sentence and turning your mind on higher,
  - make a guess that makes sense and go on to see if the sentence feels OK,
  - try out the first sounds and see if it seems like a word you know,
  - see if you understand the whole sentence, and if it's OK, keep on reading.
- If the reader is skipping or miscuing senselessly one or more words in each sentence, then the conference has to be about honestly assessing what books are good for this reader and has to end with the child reading a more appropriate book.
- Try, as often as possible, to figure out a way to keep the reader thinking through text, the way you've been working, after you leave the conference. What could he do with a friend that would extend this learning?

Interruptions and World-Building

In our collective experience before we came together, and in the data we collected together, we found that many struggling readers in our upper grade classrooms could look at text and say most of it out loud, but, when asked to retell what they had read, they appeared confused and became flustered or defensive. I had found this in my own middle school teaching, when I attempted a teacher-research study of the virtual texts (Iser, 1978) of struggling readers, that is, the text-world as the reader constructs it in her own mind. I set up my students in pairs, each with a tape recorder, and asked each pair to take turns in reader/researcher roles. The reader's job was to read the text (which I gave them) aloud and to talk when asked to. The researcher's job was to interrupt the reader every few paragraphs (sometimes at spots I'd marked in the text), to ask them to talk about what they were thinking about what they'd read, to tape what the reader said, and to try and write it all down. Since it was all pretty complicated, it took over a week to teach them to do it, and I began to be nervous about the amount of time it was requiring.

When I did start getting data from them and began examining the data, though, I was surprised to find that, after doing the study for a while, the virtual texts reported by the struggling readers were qualitatively similar to those of readers who rarely struggled. Everyone, in other words, seemed to be understanding what they were reading, even with texts I would have thought would give them trouble. The appointment to speak forced the readers to lean forward into the text and to make something of it—so that they would have something to say when it came time to speak. The interruptions broke the meaningless, perseverant decoding and required that the reader construct the text as thought. By contrast, when they read without interruptions, they allowed their gaze to glide along sentences and let the language pour over them and right off their backs without ever activating meaning. They had constructed the reading act as converting print into speech, but never into thought.

For members of our inquiry group, the think-aloud became a genre of conference in our repertoire, a basic structure on which we could improvise. We planned with the reader where she would stop and talk, then we asked her to read silently, stopping to say what she was thinking at the designated spots. Often, we'd say what *we* were thinking or wondering about, demonstrating by doing so the style of spoken thought we had in mind. If, while reading over the child's shoulder, we saw a conflict between what the reader said and our own understanding of the passage, we would point to the place we felt the conflict lay and ask something like, "What did you make of this part right here?" After a brief reasoning together about what we thought was going on, the teacher would usually say, "Well, let's see what happens," and then the student would read on. Our intention in such a conference was, even for just five or ten minutes, to support the student in moving through the piece in a fuller, richer way, surrounded by the world of the text. We thought it might provide the reader with a benchmark experience of how reading *should* feel, the sense of involvement and understanding that makes guessing what the print says an efficient process (Goodman, 1967; Smith, 1994).

We almost always tried to leave one of these interruption conferences with the student getting together with another child to keep working in the same way for a longer time. These partnerships sometimes lasted just part of that day but often became a long-term structure for that pair of readers. In the latter case, the students would choose a common text and read it together, stopping every page or so for little mini-conversations. (Short, Harste, and Burke [1996] call these little talks "say something.") Doing this over time helped more than anything else to habituate them to making meaning and released them from their tendency to process text phonologically without really thinking.

Struggling readers need both rich conversations about big ideas in texts, which let them participate as full members of a literate community, and interactions that support figuring out the details of the textual world.

Talk was the most common but not the only thinking device (Wertsch, 1991) we asked students to employ in these interruptive spaces. Sometimes we photocopied cut-up short texts, with more page breaks than the original and huge margins. With these, we asked students to read the page and to write in the white space what they were thinking before turning to the next page. Sometimes, we asked students to draw what they were seeing from time to time as they read a chapter. We also made teams of readers who, at the beginning of the reading workshop each day, would direct each other in enacting a scene from what the director had read in her book yesterday. The most important purpose of all these interruptions is not what goes on in the interruption itself, but is rather the active getting ready the reader has to accomplish internally during the reading before the predictable interruption.

In all these interruptions, if we wanted to help readers enrich the text-worlds they created in their minds, we needed to be aware of the mental actions that seem to allow readers to build worlds (Bruner, 1986). It would not help for us to insist "Build the text world!" or, worse, "Comprehend! Comprehend!" We needed to develop some more precise conceptions of the mental actions struggling readers needed to do more of.

For example, like Enciso (1992), Langer (1995), and Wilhelm (1997), we found it crucial to support readers' envisionment. Often, a reader cannot be said to be comprehending unless she is really *seeing* what the text narrates or describes. We frequently found ourselves saying "Try to picture it. What do you see?" or asking the reader to draw her image of the part she just read or to get up on her feet and show us how it went.

We also worked often with listening to the voice or sound of a text, inviting the reader to read a sentence aloud a couple of times and sound just like a news person on TV, a scary storyteller, or a narrator on a nature program, whichever voice the kid agreed was most appropriate to the text's voice. We talked about the differences among the sounds of characters' voices in stories, and we discussed whether a text felt noisy or quiet, or whether there were changes in the readers' sense of background sound between one section and the next. We found that the emphasis on listening not only enriched the narrated text-world the reader constructed but also, in evoking a stronger sense of voice, activated cueing systems associated with discourse (Bomer, 1996), genre (Pappas & Pettegrew, 1998), and syntax (Goodman, 1967), and consequently strengthened the reader's disposition toward figuring out what the words "said."

It was also useful sometimes to assist readers in bringing forward areas of knowledge they needed to be active as they read a text. Often for struggling readers, the book is way over there, distant, objective, disconnected from the known world. To bring the text closer and fit it to what's already "mine" for the reader, we worked deliberately to bring knowledge forward. If the people in a story went to a party, we talked for a few moments about parties the kid had been to. If the child were reading an article about dolphins, we would sometimes say, "Let's put the book down for a minute and just talk about dolphins. Where have you seen them before?" For the child, sharing experience and understanding with an adult makes meaning more real, more authorized and therefore more useful for the semantic cueing system. As always, to be sure that we would have accomplished more in the conference than just supporting a single reading session, we ended by thinking with the student about ways of doing independently what we had just done together.

Working with Writing

The support we provide readers to keep meaning active makes the more technical, print-focused aspects of reading more efficient (Goodman, 1967; Smith, 1994). It helps if the world and language of what they read is as close as possible to what they already know. A number of reading situations help to close that gap between active knowledge and textual meaning. It is helpful, for instance, if the reader has heard the text read aloud before. Reading a series of books with similar structures, situations, and characters helps keep formal variation and novelty to a minimum and so allows the reader to rely on past reading experiences to make sense of the present one. Language experience stories allow the reader to draw on autobiographical memory, since he was present for both the experience and the composition of the text. Surely the gap is narrowest when students read their own writing and, for that reason, we found it useful to ask struggling readers to have their writers notebooks (Bomer, 1995; Calkins, 1992) and their portfolios handy during reading time.

Sometimes, we would begin the conference by asking the student to read one of her own notebook entries, drafts, or finished pieces. Because she was reading something she wrote, she rarely if ever made non-word or syntactical miscues without self-correcting, since she knew what the text said. We could point out how strongly she monitored and self-corrected, how firmly she kept in mind what she meant, and then we could ask her to think in the same way when reading her book. Our theory was, again, that experienced struggling readers have misconceived the kind of thinking they need to do as they read. Working with their own writing allowed us to provide an experience of reading with more semantic energy and to bring that experience in close proximity to the experience of reading unfamiliar text.

The support we provide readers to keep meaning active makes the more technical, print-focused aspects of reading more efficient.

In addition to helping us assist performance, keeping student work in writing close at hand during reading conferences allowed us to assess with more accuracy and intricacy than we otherwise could have done. We could see, for instance, if readers knew letters, spelling patterns, words, sentence structures, and textual strategies, even if their oral reading performance seemed to indicate they did not. We could then see whether we needed to show them something completely new or whether we needed to work with them on applying what they knew on the run—two completely different kinds of teaching. Too often, our response to struggling readers assumes deficits that do not necessarily exist. Instead, we need to attach their reading to the strength they have already earned.

Balancing Our Conferences with Struggling Readers

The conferences I have described so far respond to struggling readers' needs for support within the reading process and the mental action of constructing textual worlds. Trouble is, those aren't the only needs they have. Like all readers, students who struggle also require support for creating a reading life, for learning craft in writing from literature, for interpretation, for questioning and critiquing the social givens in texts, for collaborating with other readers, and for other areas in which we hope students will grow. Those of us who were members of the inquiry group needed frequently to monitor ourselves by looking back through anecdotal records to make sure we were not limiting our conferences with these readers to a minimal getting-by. To read for understanding, they needed to summon all their intelligences, to bring to bear every possible kind of thinking. The more thoughts about texts readers construct, the more they define and constrain the range of possibilities as to what a particular sentence will say. We worked to make sure we had conversations with them—and they had conversations with other students—that preserved the totality of the reading act and enlarged meaning rather than holding snugly to the word and sentence level.

As we did with stronger readers, we talked with struggling readers about the ways they were composing their reading lives. We discussed their favorite places for reading, their habits of storing and carrying books, their optimal conditions for a reading session. We talked to them also about *how reading usu-*

ally goes for you, asking things like, "When you're going to read, usually, you sit down with your book and you hold it up, and then—what?" We wanted, in these conferences, to construct with the reader an awareness of how they begin the act of reading, of how they become engaged in text-supported thought. We asked, too, about the social web in which their reading life was situated—who knew what they were reading, to whom might they talk about their thinking, to and from whom they gave and received recommendations. Knowing that they needed more time and work with reading than school would provide, we thought it important for us to think with them about crafting a literate life outside of school.

In addition, we often asked questions that we hoped would lead to interpretive conversations:

- "What's grabbing your attention right now and seems important here? Why do you suppose that seems so important?"
- "What kinds of big questions are you reading with right now?"
- "What are your hunches or guesses about what the big ideas in this book might be?"
- "You're so mad about that character, I can't help but wonder if there have been times in real life when you've been so mad at someone."
- "What books or movies or TV shows have been coming to mind as you read this? Let's think about those two texts together."
- "It sounds like there might be something about fairness or justice in what you're saying about this book; what do you think?"

Interpretive response to literature like this is not something we add on after we've finished teaching "real reading"; rather, it is the essence of reading. We distort reading in perilous ways if we ignore it with *some* readers. Becoming minimally competent is not especially motivating. Without these larger, more meaningful pursuits as part of a life with reading, why bother getting better at it?

The conferring practices I have described in this article are, obviously, labor-intensive. Though they are helpful for classroom teachers in their work with students who need the most attention, one adult assisting thirty children as well as managing the entire classroom cannot provide sufficient support for children who have to move from being unable-to-read to sustaining strong readerly habits. Many of the challenges facing the children who need the most help are policy issues and not pedagogical ones. For example, agencies from the school level to the federal government might someday want to consider spending more on supporting our most vulnerable children rather than developing and mandating more tests to prove again and again these kids' difficulties making meaning of print. Regardless of decisions legislators and administrators make, however, upper grade and secondary teachers will always have struggling readers in their classes. There will always be children who make us lie awake in bed at night, who frustrate us when they will not sit still when the class is reading, who fill us with grief and rage on their behalf when we see them put their heads down during a standardized test. We will always have to do our best to teach them. Perhaps our response to these children is the test that matters most—the test of our craft, the test of our compassion and respect, the test of our intelligence, the test of our courage and hope.

Author's Note

Core members of the Teachers College Reading Project included Robin Cohen, Fran Del Monaco, Mary Kelly, Isoke Titilayo Nia, Claire Noonan, Donna Santman, Denise Sontag, and Dianne Weiss. My own work in collaboration with the group occurred in New York City classrooms where the teachers were affiliated with the Reading Project. Our work occurred within ongoing research and teaching at the Teachers College Reading Project, which I then co-directed with Lucy Calkins. Much of the work of that project was funded by Joseph Seagram & Sons. I am grateful to all those who contributed to this work, though what I write here is my own reformulation of that work, and any flaws are my responsibility.

Different members of the group, since their jobs were different, worked in the classrooms in different ways. Some members were classroom teachers, others reading teachers who worked in collaboration with classroom teachers, others administrators and staff developers who worked in a variety of ways. My own work occurred in four classrooms in two urban schools, ten visits each across eight weeks, with four follow-up visits to each classroom across another eight weeks. Two of the classroom teachers in these rooms were also in the study group. Sometimes, I conferred with my focal students while the classroom teacher conferred with others. Sometimes, especially early on, the teacher and I worked together with the focal students. Each time I was in a classroom, I also conferred with at least one student who was not one of my focal students. During every visit, I consulted with the classroom teacher, to share what I was thinking as well as to get information and advice from her/him. I should also mention that a requirement for work with our study group was that teachers had to be free to make instructional decisions in the interest of her/his students (i.e., they could not be required to use particular materials or instructional practices in order to keep their jobs) and had to be already stocked with an ample classroom library.

References

Allington, R. L. (1980). Poor readers don't get to read much in reading groups. *Language Arts, 57,* 872–877.

Atwell, N. (1986). *In the middle.* Portsmouth, NH: Heinemann.

Bomer, R. (1995). *Time for meaning: Crafting literate lives in middle and high schools.* Portsmouth, NH: Heinemann.

Bomer, R. (1996). Reading discourses: An ethnography of cohesion and difference in an urban sixth grade classroom's community of readers. Unpublished dissertation. New York: Columbia University.

Bruner, J. (1986). *Actual minds, possible worlds.* Cambridge, MA: Harvard University Press.

Calkins, L. M. (1992). *The art of teaching writing* (2nd ed.). Portsmouth, NH: Heinemann.

Cole, M. (1996). *Cultural psychology: A once and future discipline.* Cambridge, MA: Harvard University Press.

Coles, G. S. (1987). *The learning mystique: A critical look at "learning disabilities."* New York: Pantheon Books.

Edwards, D., & Mercer, N. (1987). *Common knowledge: The development of understanding in the classroom.* London: Methuen.

Enciso, P. (1992). Creating the story world: A case study of a young reader's engagement strategies and stances. In J. Many & C. Cox (Eds.), *Reader stance and literary understanding: Exploring the theories, research, and practice.* Norwood, NJ: Ablex.

George, J. C. (1959). *My side of the mountain.* New York: Dutton.

Goodman, K. (1967). Reading: A psycholinguistic guessing game. *The Journal of the Reading Specialist, 6* (4), 126–135.

Goodman, Y. (1996). *Notes from a kidwatcher: Selected writings of Yetta M. Goodman.* S. Wilde (Ed.). Portsmouth, NH: Heinemann.

Goodman, Y., & Burke, C. (1980). *Reading strategies: Focus on comprehension.* New York: Richard C. Owen.

Holt, J. (1969). *Why children fail.* London: Penguin.

Iser, W. (1978). *The act of reading: A theory of aesthetic response.* Baltimore, MD: Johns Hopkins University Press.

Langer, J. (1995). *Envisioning literature.* New York: Teachers College Press.

Lave, J., and Wenger, E. (1991). *Situated learning: Legitimate peripheral participation.* Cambridge: Cambridge University Press.

McDermott, R., & Gospodinoff, K. (1975). Social contexts for ethnic borders & school failure. In A. Wolfgang (Ed.), *Nonverbal behavior.* New York: Academic Press.

Mehan, H. (1982). The structure of classroom events and their consequences for student performance. In P. Gilmore & A. Glatthorn (Eds.), *Children in and out of school.* Washington, DC: Center for Applied Linguistics.

Pappas, C., & Pettegrew, B. (1998). The role of genre in the psycholinguistic guessing game of reading. *Language Arts, 75* (1), 36–44.

Rhodes, L., & Dudley-Marling, C. (1996). *Readers and writers with a difference: A holistic approach to teaching struggling readers and writers* (2nd ed.). Portsmouth, NH: Heinemann.

Rose, M. (1989). *Lives on the boundary.* New York: Penguin Books.

Short, K., Harste, J., & Burke, C. (1996). *Creating classrooms for authors and inquirers* (2nd ed.). Portsmouth, NH: Heinemann.

Smith, F. (1984). *Insult to intelligence: The bureaucratic invasion of our classrooms.* New York: Teachers College Press.

Smith, F. (1994). *Understanding reading: A psycholinguistic analysis of reading and learning to read* (2nd ed.). Hillsdale, NJ: Lawrence Erlbaum.

Taylor, D. (1991). *Learning denied.* Portsmouth, NH: Heinemann.

Tharp, R., & Gallimore, R. (1988). *Rousing minds to life: Teaching, learning, and schooling in social context.* Cambridge: Cambridge University Press.

Van Manen, M. (1991). *The tact of teaching: The meaning of pedagogical thoughtfulness.* Albany: State University of New York Press.

Vygotsky, L. (1962). *Thought and language.* Cambridge, MA: MIT Press.

Walmsley, S. A., & Allington, R. L. (1995). Redefining and reforming instructional support for at-risk students. In R. L. Allington (Ed.), No quick fix: *Rethinking literacy programs in America's elementary schools.* New York: Teachers College Press.

Wertsch, J. (1991). *Voices of the mind: A sociocultural approach to mediated action.* Cambridge, MA: Harvard University Press.

Wilde, S. (1992). *You kan red this.* Portsmouth, NH: Heinemann.

Wilhelm, J. (1997). *"You gotta BE the book": Teaching engaged and reflective reading with adolescents.* New York: Teachers College Press.

Wood, D., Bruner, J. S., & Ross, G. (1976). The role of tutoring in problem solving. *Journal of Child Psychology and Child Psychiatry, 17,* 89–100.

Zindel, P. (1984). *My darling, my hamburger.* New York: Bantam.

What Really Matters in Literacy Instruction?

Heidi Mills with Timothy O'Keefe

Basic skills, intensive and systematic phonics, high test scores, English only programs, discipline. Basic skills, intensive and systematic phonics, high test scores, English only programs, discipline. Basic skills, intensive and systematic phonics, high test scores, English only programs, high test scores, discipline. And so it goes. This mantra fills newspapers, school board rooms, political party headquarters, and staff development workshops. The extensive nature of current attacks on education is astonishing, shameful, and intimidating. Even the most thoughtful and successful teachers are being questioned and are questioning themselves.

Tim O'Keefe and I realize our teaching practices are certainly not yet mainstream, although we thought we had finally lived through and survived the hazards and dominance of textbook-driven curricula. Unfortunately, we once again find ourselves and colleagues across the country in the midst of professional turmoil. We are saddened by the fact that politically driven attacks on our practices have caused many of our colleagues to question their own judgment and professional autonomy. Others have retreated to the "good teaching is only safe behind closed doors" syndrome. We sincerely believe we were just beginning to access the potential of a holistic, literature-based model of instruction when our professional integrity and children's learning potential were severely undermined. In this article, Tim and I hope to remind readers why it is absolutely essential that we continue to strive for what is possible rather than retreat to what has been typical in literacy instruction.

Tim and I have been working together in various parts of the country for eighteen years. Most recently, we have been collaborating with a group of remarkable colleagues at the Center for Inquiry, a small public school of choice in Columbia, South Carolina. Tim is the second/third grade teacher there and I

Heidi Mills is a Professor in the Department of Instruction and Teacher Education at the University of South Carolina. **Tim O'Keefe** is an elementary teacher at the Center for Inquiry in Columbia, South Carolina.

am a member of the University of South Carolina curriculum-research team. Before opening the Center for Inquiry, I spent one day a week for eight years living and learning in several of Tim's classrooms, exploring how children learn language and mathematics within the context of a holistic, inquiry-based curriculum. The classrooms featured in this piece represent a range of districts and learners. However, they are all united by a teacher who carefully creates curriculum by looking closely and listening carefully to his students. I hope to challenge the restricted vision of education portrayed in public venues by inviting readers into the thoughtful learning communities Tim has built and, in so doing, reframe what counts by examining what matters first.

Fundamental Beliefs that Inform Our Practices

As holistic educators, we ground our literacy instruction in powerful pieces of literature, writers notebooks and frequent, focused learning rituals built upon reflection and conversations about the learning process. As we consider the essential features of thoughtful classroom engagements that are anchored in writing and talking about children's literature, it is the general stance we take as teachers and learners that makes the difference. We have learned to critique our classroom dialogue by asking whether or not our literature study group discussions reflect the passion, interest, and commitment we find in adult reading guilds (Short & Harste with Burke, 1996).

We understand that as teachers we have the right and responsibility to provide intentional, thoughtful instruction within the context of literacy engagements, but we must do so carefully so as not to "basalize" the experience. While Tim provides daily opportunities for children to *learn about language*, he does not frame such discussions around powerful literature in contrived or artificial ways. Instead, he creates a balanced daily schedule or curricular framework so that children will *learn language, learn about language and learn through language* each day (Halliday, 1982). Children learn language as they use it for various purposes; they learn about language as they consciously reflect upon its processes, skills, and concepts; and they learn through language by exploring content across disciplines via oral and written language. Tim accomplishes this balance by creating a daily schedule that includes demonstrations, engagements, reflection, and celebration:

- Demonstrations of language, skills, concepts, and strategies in use;
- Extensive opportunities to engage in uninterrupted reading, writing and conversation;
- Individual, small group and whole class reflection sessions;
- Daily opportunities to celebrate accomplishments with others in the classroom or school.

This curricular framework reflects our belief that children learn best when skills and strategies are taught within the context of authentic literacy engagements (Avery, 1995; Freppon & Dahl, 1991). In so doing, we create curriculum *with* and *for* children (Mills, O'Keefe, & Stephens, 1992). Our learners are provided opportunities to intentionally and systematically uncover the skills, strategies, and concepts that accomplished readers and writers understand and use.

We have successfully taught children to read and write while using reading and writing to learn (Short & Pierce, 1990).

Tim and I realize that it takes a tremendous knowledge base, and a great deal of thought, planning, reflection, and revision to truly operationalize these beliefs. In fact, we agree with Jerome Harste (1997) when he suggests that it is a lot easier to make a classroom look holistic than it is to make it sound holistic. It is not enough to purchase tables or move desks together, to bring in high-quality children's literature, to publish children's writing, and to encourage children to talk about and/or write about books. It is the *stance* we take as teachers toward texts, knowledge, learning, other learners, and our role in the world that makes the critical difference. And because of this stance, our children's insights, ideas, questions, poems, and stories are heard, valued, and used as both anchors and springboards for curriculum development.

Valuing the Informative and Transformative Role of Literature

Before we share the engagements that frame our reading and writing instruction, it is important to look closely and listen carefully as Tim O'Keefe leads a literature discussion. We begin with the "talk" because we have found that the ways in which the teacher interacts with the children and the sense of community that pervades the classroom profoundly influence the moment-by-moment incidents that make or break a strategy lesson, classroom ritual, or evaluation device.

We join Tim's third grade class immediately following the reading of two books from an intergenerational text set. On this particular day, he chose The Sunshine Home (1994) by Eve Bunting and The Sunsets of Miss Olivia Wiggins (1998) by Lester Laminack. It was late in the year, which meant that Tim had already negotiated the structure of the day with his children. It was decided early in the year that whole group responses to literature were most engaging when the children had some uninterrupted, yet focused time to respond through sketching or writing before talking. Reflective writing or sketching in response to powerful literature had become a habit of the heart and mind for this group. This plan encouraged more children to participate because they had time to think about individual insights, questions, and connections that would then be woven into the fabric of the conversation. In fact, the group developed a shared code or shorthand ("lessons and connections") that they often accessed when interpreting texts. They found common themes such as the search for personal connections, connections across literature, and the identification of lessons learned to be useful lenses when responding to literature.

Lovely classical music filled the room as the children wrote and wrote and wrote. While there was a predictable structure to literature study, the class was so connected that Tim simply "read" the group to determine when they were ready to return to the carpet for their shared book talk. When he noticed that most of the children were finished writing or sketching, he changed the music to signify the transition to the whole group gathering area in the classroom.

Tim opened the conversation by saying, "Who would like to start us off in this discussion? Remember, you don't have to read your notes, you may just want to have your notes in front of you and say what's on your mind."

Suzannah began by reading her written reflection: "This story really makes me think a lot about my grandma who died in a hospital and how things would have been if she was still alive." She paused, eyes glancing down her paper, then continued, "And, uh, Eve Bunting is one of the best writers. She can experience love and sadness and hope in her stories. And to do that is one of the best gifts in the world."

Tim responded, "Nice comments. One of the things I wonder is how an author can do that? How can an author move you to tears in just a few words? Edward, your go."

> *We were just beginning to access the potential of a holistic, literature-based model of instruction when our professional integrity and children's learning potential were severely undermined.*

Edward responded, "Connections and lessons. I learned that some grandmas and grandpas live in nursing homes and some don't. And my favorite part was when Mrs. Nelson was puzzled and said, 'Was that the boy that came in just a minute ago?'"

Tim said, "So you liked the humor in the story too. And it's nice that she put some humor in there, 'cause if it was all sort of sad, if it was all the same emotion, I don't think it would be such an interesting book. So the little things around the edges of the story make a big difference."

Rebecca inquired, "I wonder if Miss Olivia had some kind of memory or thinking disease since she didn't talk or anything. And if she did, I wonder what the disease was?"

Tim responded, "Do you remember the dedication in Lester's book?"

"I think it was his grandmother. She died of Alzheimer's disease."

"I think he was describing her as having Alzheimer's disease—where she is apparently able to think about things but really can't say them."

Several children chimed in, "It's a really bad disease. Some people die from it."

Tim paused and spoke softly, "Both of my wife's grandparents had that before they eventually died."

Aaron was next to speak, "Well, one of my connections is that you see these two books remind me of when I go and see my grandpa. And a lesson was that you don't have to be afraid to go into a nursing home because no one is going to hurt you and nothing is going to happen to you. Um, and it was kind of scary for me but then I got kind of used to it and then I wasn't as scared. And, my feelings about this were both sad because you could feel how they would be in both books. And I know what it was like."

Tim reacted warmly, "So you can relate to it personally, can't you?"

Matt said, "I think it just made you think about how the people felt in the nursing home and the people visiting there. How they felt. 'Cause I'm thinking that Gram in the *Sunshine Home,* all she usually had to talk to were other old people in the nursing home and the nurses that didn't know about her life before she was in the nursing home."

Rosa jumped in, "I sometimes get butterflies in my stomach when I go to places like Vancouver where my granny lives. It was the first time for me to see her. I didn't know whether to back off or to take my chances. I took a risk. Once I knew her a little more, I did the same with my grandpa."

Tim asked, "Are you glad you took that risk?"

"Yeah."

Robert joined the conversation. "This sort of goes with Aaron's. I wonder why whenever Tim went to see his grandma, he was afraid to go in?"

Tim asked, "Do you have any thoughts about why he might have been afraid?"

Edward responded, "I have two things to share. Probably he thought that his grandma might not have been able to talk or anything and he might have been afraid to see her."

Tim added, "Afraid that she had changed so strongly."

"And I bet that Eve Bunting and Lester are serious writers. 'Cause they both write about serious things."

And so it went. The conversation continued for some time, with the children and teacher building on, confirming, and sometimes revising each others' ideas.

Reflecting on the Book Talk

When carefully analyzing the children's written responses and the conversation that followed, we found patterns that reflected the essence of literature study. This particular literacy engagement sounds much more like an adult reading guild than a formal lesson designed to teach reading. However, we have become quite passionate about the need for engagements that inform and transform children as readers, writers, and members of a democratic society. The children in this classroom learned the skills and strategies that count in elementary school. In fact, their standardized test scores were quite high. Most important, though, they learned what really mattered in literacy (Stephens, 1990). They did so in part because of their exposure to and interaction with high-quality children's literature. The books mattered a great deal, but good books alone are not enough. It is how we situate ourselves in relation to the books, how we juxtapose the books in relation to other texts we have encountered, and how the teacher and children co-create individual and shared interpretations of the texts. The teacher and the teaching make a critical difference. We have learned that it is essential that the teacher

- appreciates the power of story as a universal way of knowing and communicating.
- understands that learning begins with personal connections and interpretations of text. Comprehension is assumed while interpretation of the texts is explicitly encouraged.

- allows stories to grow out of stories. The children tell stories to explain and extend the meanings being constructed by individuals and the group as a whole.
- realizes that multiple perspectives are best uncovered through conversations as all members of the learning community share stories, personal experiences, and significant memories.
- allows new ideas to be born, refined, and revised as children make connections with others' contributions.
- values the way genuine conversations promote a sense of wonder and encourage children to make predictions, to identify lessons learned and knowledge gained.
- participates in conversations by naturally validating, supporting, and extending ideas generated by the group.
- promotes inquiry and co-creates curriculum with the children so that humaness is acknowledged and celebrated. The literacy endeavors begin, evolve, and end at the heart of things . . . what really matters.
- honors literature and accesses it as a tool for informing and transforming our understanding of ourselves, each other, and the world.

The previous conversation illuminates the ways in which the children used language and literature as tools for learning. They explored the writing strategies each author employed, analyzed critical issues in aging and inter-generational relationships, considered and/or reconsidered personal relationships with their own grandparents, and so on. The texts, reading, writing, and dialogue worked in concert to ensure that all who entered into the experience left as different readers, writers, and members of their classroom and family communities.

The Habit of Kidwatching

Teaching from a holistic, literature-based perspective seems so simple and logical on one hand yet so complex, demanding, and compelling on the other. There are so many choices, children, good books, strategies, and skills to uncover, and learning communities to be built. Many teachers wonder how teachers like Tim make curricular decisions. What makes the critical difference? Put another way, what is truly basic? For us, kidwatching (Goodman, 1978) is at the heart of it all. Intensive and extensive kidwatching is central to Tim's instruction and evaluation. He can teach responsively because he truly knows his children. Such responsive teaching leads to intimate instruction. As Ayers (1993) suggests, to make learning genuine, it must be intimate. The information Tim gathers and interprets through his daily kidwatching rituals allows him to make informed instructional decisions.

From Kidwatching to Curriculum: Strategy-Sharing Sessions

Children in Tim's classroom function as teachers as well as learners. Tim builds time into the daily schedule to highlight strategies he notices children using effectively and to provide opportunities for the children to reflect upon and make explicit the skills and strategies they find especially useful when reading and writing. These strategy-sharing sessions are quite generative. The children who present a strategy must consciously reflect upon and explain their thinking, which often leads to greater depth and breadth in the quality of the original idea. Additionally, their young colleagues often make connections with their own habits and share similar stories or variations on the theme. The teacher talks too and, in so doing, offers his personal experience and expertise regarding the concept, skill, or strategy.

Tim formally invites individuals to highlight their work while also providing the group with ownership of this process. When children recognize that they have an insight to share with their young colleagues, they simply sign the strategy-sharing list posted on the board each day. Due to the predictable class schedule, the children know they will be invited to share strategies immediately following literature study and writing workshop.

Reflecting on Reading Strategies

While Tim has found whole group and small group discussions essential in his teaching, he has also come to believe that it is crucial to get to know each child well as a reader. To do so, he began conducting regular individual conferences during literature study time. He calls this time "coaching." During "coaching," he meets with individual readers and asks them to read from the book they are in the midst of exploring individually or with a group. He takes thorough notes regarding the children's miscues and reading strategies, makes general comments about the children's competence and confidence with the text and the students' reflections on their reading strategies. He uses this time to provide focused support for individual readers by validating effective strategies and making recommendations that will promote growth. Additionally, Tim uses the data he gathers from individual coaching to share important insights with the whole class during strategy-sharing sessions. In this way, he attends to individual needs and interests while also gathering information that will be instrumental in fostering growth in the class at large.

Sharing Reading Strategies

After "coaching" third grader Sana as she read and reflected on *Shiloh* (1991) by Phyllis Reynolds Naylor, Tim asked Sana for permission to share some of the ideas they discussed during the "coaching" session with the class for their daily strategy-sharing ritual. Given that it was an honor to be featured during strategy-sharing sessions, Sana agreed without hesitation. At the close of literature study, the children met on the carpet to share their progress within and across literature study groups. Next, Tim said that he wanted to highlight some of the things he noticed Sana doing as she read and discussed *Shiloh*.

Tim began, "I noticed that the unusual grammar in the story didn't phase Sana. She read fluently. To me, it was a sign that she was truly immersed in the story and had learned to think and speak like the characters in the story. In fact, when I asked her to reflect on what she found interesting in the story, she said she liked the 'old timey language.' What a nice way to put it! It is the special language or dialect in good books that makes the characters come alive and give the story its color and shape."

Next, Tim told the class that Sana identified some words she found fascinating. She looked for words the author used effectively. Tim invited her to
share by saying, "Sana, tell us what you thought about the word 'slinks.'"

Using her hands to show the motion, she said she figured out that "It must
mean duck down and go away because that is what would work in the story. I
also had a little trouble with the word 'pneumonia'. I knew that 'p' and 'n'
don't usually go together and so I had to use what was around the word, I
mean knowing that someone was really sick. I paused and thought about it
and then remembered that it must be pneumonia and so I didn't need to make
the 'p' sound."

To close the strategy-sharing session, Tim invited Sana to share how she had
changed as a reader. Sana knew Tim was going to ask her to share such thoughts
so she read her written reflection entitled "How I've Changed as a Reader":

> I've been reading so much faster than the beginning of the year. So far I've
> read three chapter books. I've been learning a lot from reading. From reading,
> I've learned that whales used to live on land. I've been learning harder words
> like for example "enthusiastically." I'm using different strategies for reading
> like looking at the pictures and the words close to it and not using simple
> "sounding out". Sometimes I use the reading strategies for writing to help me
> figure how to spell words.

Before Sana had a chance to sit back down, her young colleagues started
making connections between their own reading habits and the ideas she men-
tioned. Tim reviewed the big ideas Sana demonstrated, such as reading fluently and attending to the beauty and uniqueness of the dialect in the text; and
using what you know about the world, what is happening in the story, the
word that would make the most sense in the sentence, and phonics knowledge
to figure out unknown words.

Tim thanked her for sharing with the class. Everyone applauded in concert, and Tim introduced the next event. This brief yet predictable feature of
the curriculum fostered self-reflection that led the children to analyze and gain
control over their own strategies while also helping others become accomplished
readers and writers.

Sharing Writing Strategies

The strategy-sharing session that follows emerged in the same third grade
classroom immediately following writing workshop. Zac began, "Okay, the
strategy I did today, so I would get my train of thought started, I read over my
piece before I started writing."

Tim validated and extended this notion by responding, "How many of the
rest of you do that? It is a great idea and I always do that even when I am
reading to get into the train of thought as Zac said. Great idea, Zac!"

The whole class admired Zac for his idea because they all knew it was often
difficult for him to find his stride as a writer during workshop. He sensed the
group's respect and sighed as he returned to his circle of friends on the floor.

Frances made her way to the front of the group and began, "If I didn't
know how to spell a word I would look it up in the dictionary or ask someone
how to spell a word."

Tim reacted, "All right! Another good strategy." Looking to the group he continued, "Any other strategies for words when you are not sure how to spell it?"

Shelby said, "When I self-edit it, I, um, I circle it."

Tim inquired, "So when you write it you circle it and when you go back over it you see if it looks right?" She nods.

Robert chimed in, "Sometimes when I come to a word I am not sure of I just break it up into parts."

Tim responded, "So you spell one word part at a time?"

Rachael added, "I write it on the side three times and then whichever one looks the best I put it down but I still circle it just in case."

Tim verified the usefulness of using visual memory while also giving Zac credit for spreading the good word. He said, "That's what we called Zac's strategy at the beginning of last year."

It is absolutely essential that we continue to strive for what is possible rather than retreat to what has been typical in literacy instruction.

Zac reacted sincerely with "But I learned it from you."

Phillip jumped up and spread his arms open wide to demonstrate his strategy. "Sometimes let's say if there is a word in a sentence I don't know it's like let's see." He pointed to a spot in the air and asked, "OK, what's that word? OK, I'll come back to you. 'Blank' is where sun makes life for plants." He pointed to a spot in the air for each word as he said it. He looked down to his friends at his feet and continued, "That gives me a clue because I remember my dad told me that word was 'photosynthesis.' Because I know what it means then I can use the words around it [acting it out in the air] to help me."

I was videotaping and chimed in, "That makes sense to use the words around it to figure out what it means."

Tim added, "That is really a reading strategy, isn't it?"

Phillip interrupted by saying, "Besides, that is also connected. You see if you know how to read better, you also know how to write better because you know how to write those words because you have read those words."

Tim smiled and said, "No kidding! The better reader you are, the better writer. And the better writer you are, the better reader you are. Good connection."

It was Tim's turn. He followed the pattern established by the class. "The strategy I would like to share is about making paragraphs, going down to the next line and indenting five spaces or so. Robert, may I share your autobiography?"

Robert beamed. "Sure!"

"OK, as I read along, if you think the sentence I start belongs in a new paragraph, why don't you give me the thumb up. Of course, the first sentence you write will be in a new paragraph so you will indent." Tim began reading and the children listened carefully, responding each time the subject in Robert's text changed. After completing the autobiography, they reflected on why they made the decisions they did, and summarized important points to remember about making paragraphs.

The third graders featured in this conversation had the privilege of working with the same teacher for two years through a looping organizational structure. On this particular day they learned a strategy for reconnecting to a work in progress; various spelling strategies (self-editing, using a dictionary, asking an expert, using visual memory, breaking words into syllables); the value of skipping an unknown word and using context clues to figure it out; and the importance of reading like a writer and writing like a reader.

The richness of this learning ritual takes on new meaning when we multiply the insights shared during this single event by three hundred and sixty days. The opportunity to live and learn together intensively and extensively for two school years resulted in children who, by traditional standardized tests as well as holistic measures, became accomplished readers and writers.

The Universal Nature of Good Teaching: Strategy Sharing Across Contexts

Tim has come to believe that he is at his best as a teacher when he can *teach out of and into* children's immediate work. The previous classroom example featured a few specific strategies that were on the teacher's and third graders' minds at that particular point in time and Tim employed the same reflective device with other classes. The cultural, economic, ethnic, and academic groups Tim has worked with over time have varied from school to school, yet Tim's beliefs about teaching and learning have been anchored in a transactional/ holistic model of literacy. Although the content in the explicit curriculum changed from district to district and grade level to grade level, he found that teaching practices such as strategy-sharing sessions supported all learners all of the time.

When Tim taught transition-first-grade he spent a great deal of time helping children learn letter sound relationships. He intentionally and systematically highlighted the role of phonics in reading and writing so that the children would come to understand and use the graphophonic cue system effectively. Tim puts it this way: "While graphophonemic relationships are highlighted in my classroom, I make an effort to get children to focus on the multiple cue systems available to them, for no cue system by itself is sufficient for effective communication. To the students in my class, letter sounds were only one way of supporting the meaning-making process, and it only worked when used in concert with other cue systems" (Mills, O'Keefe, & Stephens, 1992, p. 1).

Phonics instruction often involved making the children's implicit understandings explicit. While Tim planned demonstration lessons and literacy engagements that foregrounded consistencies and inconsistencies in letter sound relationships, the formal mini-lessons did not follow any predetermined, artificial sequence. Instead, he looked to the children to determine when, how, and why he should address particular skills and strategies. He created a curricular framework that ensured daily opportunities for children to have *direct experi-*

ences with language skills and strategies, and he employed kidwatching strategies to determine which individuals, small groups, and the whole class might benefit from it the most. In this way, the curriculum was shaped and reshaped by each new insight or question.

Time for strategy sharing was built into the daily schedule much like it is in Tim's third grade classroom today. In the transition-first-grade classroom, Tim found that it worked best to use brief yet focused texts rather than powerful children's literature or even the children's personal narrative texts for whole class reflection sessions. Tim used predictable books or pattern books to feature language concepts, conventions, skills, and effective reading strategies as tools to teach children to read. After reading a predictable book together as a class, the teacher and children often discussed letter pattern relationships, words they recognized, the punctuation used, the pictures, and the strategies they used to make, confirm, or revise predictions. Tim wanted the children to first enjoy the story and construct meaning from the text. Then he used the same familiar pattern book to help the children develop a knowledge base about the ways in which letters, words, illustrations, and texts are structured.

As teachers, we have the right and responsibility to provide intentional, thoughtful instruction within the context of literacy engagements, but we must do so carefully so as not to "basalize" the experience.

Tim established a class ritual of reflecting on entries from the daily class calendar to foreground phonics generalizations and other skills and concepts. For instance, when six-year-old Tony wrote a message on the class calendar to permanently record an important event in his learning history, he said, "I'm making a book." He spelled three out of four words conventionally and explained to the group that he simply remembered how to spell the word *book* from reading it. This explanation illustrated that he used visual memory as a primary strategy. When Tim asked him to share his thinking regarding *making*, which he spelled *macking*, he explained, "I've seen you put *ck* on the end of words. Then I just wrote the *m* and the *a* by listening to the sounds and then I wrote the *ing*," showing a sensitivity to common letter patterns in words.

"How did you know the *ing*?" Tim asked.

Tony answered quite matter-of-factly, "You taught me that they go together."

Tim noted that Tony demonstrated his understanding that *ck* and *ing* go together. He simply overgeneralized the *ck* in this instance. He also stated that he figured out the beginning of the word, *ma*, by listening to the sounds. Tony's explanation highlighted how he used multiple strategies to construct and share meaning (Mills, O'Keefe, & Stephens, 1992).

Strategy-sharing sessions such as these are used to publicly recognize children's effective use of skills and strategies. Tim's careful kidwatching allows him to *teach into and out of* children's needs and interests and, in so doing, he validates, expands, and fine-tunes children's competence while building their confidence as language users.

When Teachers and Parents Become Kidwatching Partners

During eighteen years of teaching, Tim has taught preschool through sixth grade in four states. While the political times and specific teaching contexts have varied tremendously over time and space, he has consistently been provided professional autonomy. As we reflected upon this fact, we wondered why he could teach in ways that were consistent with his beliefs when so many of his colleagues were required to "follow the book." We first thought that it was because of his commitment to his beliefs. However, in these political times, some of the most passionate and knowledgeable teachers are being denied access to information regarding holistic instruction and are being monitored carefully to make sure they "are true to the new party line," which often means using intensive and systematic phonics. So, how can we learn from our past to deal effectively with the present and our future?

As we took a second, closer look at the support Tim has received for his instruction, we realized that he establishes an intimate, collaborative relationship with his children's parents, just as he does with his students. In other words, he holds the same model when working with parents that he employs day in and day out with their children. He extends an open invitation for parents to visit, work, live, and learn in his room. He also writes extensive narrative reports each grading period whether or not he also has to respond using traditional letter grades. Such efforts, while essential, do not alter the hierarchy that is often established between teachers *who know* and parents *who care*. The single most effective engagement Tim has devised over the years to promote genuine collaboration with his children's parents emerged when he began incorporating parents' insights and questions into his weekly newsletters.

Tim sends a newsletter home every Wednesday. He usually begins each letter by sharing news from the classroom. He weaves in his philosophical position by "showing " and interpreting the children's work. The focus is always on the children and the rich learning taking place in the classroom. The parents, who know and care deeply about their children's growth and happiness, are delighted about the learning invitations and evaluation strategies simply because they make sense when presented in this way. He does not compare his teaching approaches against a mainstream norm. Instead, he illuminates the worth of using children's literature and authentic writing projects by featuring the children's insights, and accomplishments.

Tim has also adapted the same reflective engagements that work in the classroom for use in the newsletter. He extends an invitation to parents each week to engage their child(ren) in the same kinds of activities the children use during literature study, writing, and math workshop. Tim begins with a demonstration using an artifact from the children just as he does when presenting a new skill, strategy, or concept in the classroom. Next, he invites the parents to use the 3+'s and a wish format when interpreting their children's response to the activity (Mills & Clyde, 1990). In so doing, he has invited the parents into his "kidwatching club" by explicitly valuing their insights and questions. Finally, he fosters collaborative and informative conversations among parents by publishing their written comments in the next newsletter. He validates their ideas, insights, and concerns just as he does their children's and lets them know that their wishes become goals for him instructionally. This strategy allows the parents' voices to be heard and valued and provides the opportunity for parents to teach each other as well. He earns their trust and respect because he has learned how to hold his model with all learners, tall and small.

Newsletter, 11/12/97

Dear Parents,

Things have been going great in the third grade. Over the last two weeks, as you must know, we have been doing quite a lot with our literature study of *Charlotte's Web*. Someone asked the other day, "Mr. O'Keefe, will we be doing *Charlotte's Web* all year?" The answer is NO but what we have done with it has far exceeded my expectation. The children have really developed as readers and writers through this book. Most children became very good at writing and responding to literature. The literature discussions were priceless. Several children got the chance to lead discussions and everyone rose to the occasion. Even children who hardly ever speak out in class were wonderful at leading the small group discussions of this marvelous book.

Thanks to the Mehmood's for loaning us the video. The children had the unique opportunity to see the film just after reading the book and the comparisons were great. To top it off, the play at the Township Auditorium, while different, was also enjoyable and gave us yet another look at this great story. We have created a three way diagram to compare and contrast the three versions of the story. The children wrote papers comparing the film and book. There are almost constant connections to the story throughout the day. Ahhh! It's a good feeling when something comes together as nicely as this literary unit has.

I want to thank you for the responses to the written conversations about the story. The children and you wrote such wonderful, thought provoking questions. The depth and clarity of the responses was great. Am I wrong, or did I spot some tear stains on the papers? Some of the connections to other books and people in your lives made your written conversations exciting to read. Many of your papers were so personal that it felt like I was eavesdropping on an intimate conversation.

Your comments about your child as a reader were right on target. Some of your comments are listed below:

> Thomas is very good at understanding the meaning of words he's not familiar with. He uses the context of the sentence to help learn the meaning of the new word . . . He got into the emotions of the story and identified with how Wilbur felt about Charlotte . . . Reginald is getting more out of stories. Not only is he reading better, he's listening to what he's reading . . . Each character had a different voice or timing . . . She has a good use of emotion when she sees the exclamation marks . . . She brings interest and excitement by changing her voice when reading different characters and displaying different sentiments . . . She's

learning to inject emotion into what she is reading . . . I've noticed improvement in his retention as well as relating what he reads to other stories and events . . . Reading this chapter together led into some healthy discussion of life, death and friendships . . . He is reading new words and building endurance to read longer . . . He gets a real kick out of the funny parts and really "feels" the sad parts . . . She can discuss what she reads and writes about it confidently . . .

There were so many excellent comments and observations from you. I continue to be impressed about you as "Kidwatchers." Of course, there were many wishes for your children as well. Your wishes for your child as a reader become my goals. Your feedback is so important. I know it takes a lot of time to complete an assignment like this but your work makes such an important difference.

We will be reading another chapter book as a class. The books is *Shiloh* by Phyllis Reynolds Naylor. It is a wonderful story about a child and his relationships with an animal and his family. There are lots of lessons in the story. I'm sure that you would like to read it along with your child. If you were able to keep up in the book, you could have some wonderful literature discussions at home. I'll let you know the cost as soon as I contact the bookstore. If you have the book at home, let me know so that I can order the right number for our class.

The field trip to see *CW* was a nice success due, in large part, to the parents who came along. Our sincere thanks to Katy and Gary Hassen, Rubina Mehmood, Susan Bergmann, Claudia Johnson, Lark Francis, Karen Colburn, and Frankie McLean. It is so nice to have such a supportive group of parents along.

This week's newsletter assignment is for the children to complete the multiplication problems created in class. These demonstrate that the children really DO know what multiplication is and how it is used in a practical way in our daily lives to figure out real problems. Most of these stories involve multiple sets but a few deal with arrays (rows and columns). The children are supposed to write an **equation** for the stories and solve them. Everyone knows that they also need to write the **units** for each problem by their answers. As always, your comments to me about how your child did on this assignment would be helpful. Let's have these completed by Monday.

That's all for now. Thanks for reading and thanks for all you do!!

Tim

Each day I wourk for six min. :
I get $7.00 for a min. How mouch
do I make? Phillip

When What Matters Counts

Teaching during these political times can be discouraging when best practices are under constant attack by politicians and the media. As educators, we are constantly reminded that we must focus on basic skills, in other words, on *what counts*. However, the teacher and children featured in this piece have very different notions about teaching and learning than those often found on editorial pages in newspapers. It is my hope that our profession will continue to look closely and listen carefully within the walls of our classrooms. In so doing, I am confident the children will simply remind us that *what matters* is really *what counts*.

References

Avery, C. (1995). *And with a light touch*. Portsmouth, NH: Heinemann.

Ayers, W. (1993). *To teach: The journey of a teacher*. New York: Teachers College Press.

Bunting, E. (1994). *Sunshine Home*. New York: Clarion Books.

Freppon, P., & Dahl, K. (1991). "Learning about phonics in a whole language classroom." *Language Arts, 68,* 190–197.

Goodman, Y. (1978). Kidwatching: An alternative to testing. *Journal of National Elementary School Principals, 57* (4): 22–27.

Halliday, M. (1982). Three aspects of children's language development: Learning language, learning through language, learning about language. In *Oral and written language development research,* edited by Y. Goodman, M.H. Haussler, and D. Strickland, 7–19. Urbana, IL: National Council of Teachers of English.

Harste, J. (1997). Semiotics and educational change. Speech at the International Reading Association Preconference Institute on Inquiry. Atlanta, GA.

Laminack, L. (1998). *The sunsets of Miss Olivia Wiggins*. Atlanta, GA: Peachtree Publishers.

Mills, H., & Clyde, J. A. (Eds.). (1990). *Portraits of whole language classrooms*. Portsmouth, NH: Heinemann.

Mills, H., O'Keefe, T., & Stephens, D. (1992). *Looking closely: Exploring the role of phonics in one whole language classroom.* Urbana, IL: National Council of Teachers of English.

Naylor, P. (1991). *Shiloh.* New York: Bantam Doubleday Dell.

Short, K., & Harste, J., with Burke, C. (1996). *Creating classrooms for authors and inquirers.* Portsmouth, NH: Heinemann.

Short, K., & Pierce, K. (Eds.). (1990). *Talking about books.* Portsmouth, NH: Heinemann.

Stephens, D. (Ed.). (1990). *What matters: A primer for teaching reading.* Portsmouth, NH: Heinemann.

Editors' Note: The Children's Voices section in this issue features the reflective writing of Tim's students as they responded to *The Sunshine Home* (Bunting, 1994) and *The Sunsets of Miss Olivia Wiggins* (Laminack, 1998).

Skilled or Skillful:
What's the Difference for Readers?

Carol Gilles with Jean Dickinson

Mrs. Miller and Ms. Smith are hard-working, dedicated professionals who engage their students in the study of literature. Both are well-respected teachers who want their students to be proficient readers who love literature. Both attend in-service meetings and occasionally take a class from a local university. And yet, their practices in the name of literature study are vastly different.

Students in Mrs. Miller's sixth grade class engage in literature study by self-selecting books within a choice of four—*Tuck Everlasting* (Babbitt, 1975), *White Lilacs* (Meyer, 1993), *Music of Dolphins* (Hesse, 1996), and *Song of the Trees* (Taylor, 1975). They read the books individually and jot down responses in their literature logs to bring up in the discussion. Their teacher often circulates while students read silently, checking on their progress and offering strategies. When students meet in a small group, the teacher is often present. In the group they talk about the book by connecting to it and examining how the book can illuminate their lives. The teacher is an important part of these discussions: nudging here, asking an "I wonder" question there. Often students complete self-designed projects that deepen their experience with the books and cause them to reflect about how they have changed based on the books they have read and shared. Finally, they complete a self-evaluation.

Two miles down the road, Ms. Smith's sixth grade students are also engaged in the study of literature. All of these students are reading the same book, *Tuck Everlasting* (Babbitt, 1975), and Ms. Smith has purchased the Skill Masters from the Teachers' Store. After each reading assignment, the students are asked to complete a certain number of skill pages. Many of the skills covered are those of alphabetizing, recognizing vocabulary words, and putting

---

Carol Gilles is an Assistant Professor in the Department of Curriculum and Instruction at the University of Missouri. She is co-editor (with Kathryn Mitchell Pierce) of *Cycles of Meaning* (Heinemann, 1993). **Jean Dickinson** teaches in a fifth-sixth multiage classroom in Cherokee Trail School in Parker, Colorado.

events in order. Ms. Smith has the children mark each others' packets as she repeats the correct answer. The answers sometimes lead to a whole group discussion, but typically the same five or six students talk and the others are quiet. The final page of the skill packet is a multiple-choice test, which each child takes. The scores are merged with individual page scores and a final grade is given.

The connotation of "skill" has changed from something that one possesses . . . to a narrowly defined set of procedures and information usually put together for teachers by a distant publisher. . . .

The practices of these two teachers reflect the recent talk about literature-based reading programs and the teaching of skills. Some teachers worry that they are not directly teaching skills in literature study, yet their students are asked to master certain skills for testing. Others find themselves criticized because they are bringing too many skills into literature discussion groups. In this article, we contrast skills and the notion of being skillful; explore why there is such a commotion about the teaching of direct skills; articulate procedures and structures inherent in literature study that help students become more skillful interpreters and readers; and, finally, detail the role of the teacher in helping students become skillful.

As a starting point, the *Webster's Dictionary* (1991) definition of skill is worth noting:

> Skill: (n.) 2) The ability to use one's knowledge effectively and readily in execution or performance; proficiency, dexterity, 3) a learned power of doing a thing competently; a developed aptitude or ability. SYN see ART. (p. 1104)
> Skill—Archaic: To make a difference (Webster's, 1967, p. 815)

Think of how *skill* is used in all circles except education: a skilled carpenter, a skillful physician, a lawyer who uses his knowledge of the law and skill as a speaker to free his client. Somewhere in the last twenty years, the connotation of skill changed from something that one possesses (as in "he is a skilled craftsman") to a narrowly defined set of procedures and information usually put together for teachers by a distant publisher (as in "complete your skill-pack for *Tuck Everlasting*").

Mrs. Miller's and Ms. Smith's practices reflect these different views of skills. Ms. Smith's practice reflects a "sub-skills" model. She requires her students to know time-honored concepts (such as main idea, alphabetizing, and sequencing) because these items are deemed important—they are tested at the end of the skill-packs, and on many state tests. Worksheets give her the confidence that these items will be "directly taught," using some of the words from the story being read, and that important skills haven't been overlooked. Reading the book gives students practice in reading and a place to apply those things they have learned in the skill-sheets. She trusts that if children are taught these basic skills, they will be able to pass the tests; the completed worksheets are a measure of her accountability. Pierce (1990) reminds us that sometimes skills become an issue because they represent a standard against which teachers and students are measured, rather than because the skills are important to readers.

Mrs. Miller agrees that skills are important. However, her primary focus is to engage the students in an experience that can help them understand more about humanity and their own lives. She knows that, as students discuss the story, they will by necessity use skills, such as connecting events to their own lives, putting events in sequence, or identifying traits of characters in order to ask and answer their own questions about the story—for example, Why doesn't the family let the White men buy their land in *Song of the Trees* (Taylor, 1975)? To answer this question, posed by a peer, students have to think deeply about the character traits of the family. Barnes (1995) reminds us that children's language and thinking are developed not through isolated activities that are highly abstract and hold little meaning for them, but in "the service of *their* purposes" (p. 4). Thus a "skill" or "strategy" may be learned best as the student uses it in order to talk about something he/she has deemed important. Students use the skill in the service of their own learning and in the process learn more about the book, about the reading process, about literary terms, and about themselves as readers.

Literature study groups offer a context in which students can use their knowledge about the topic, their understandings about the book, and their abilities to discuss to create meanings together effectively and readily. Within the context of literature study, teachers help students be more efficient, proficient, and skillful readers. They encourage them to draw on their backgrounds of experience; demonstrate how to form, consider, and pose questions; and enable them to see the power of literature in illuminating their lives.

This scenario of learning is different from a dependence on skill-packs, depicted by Ms. Smith's practices, where the exercises are decontextualized. Activities from skill-packs, such as matching vocabulary words from the story to their meanings, sequencing events in the story, and filling in problem-solution charts are ends in themselves. They rarely connect to the intentions, knowledge, or questions of the learners.

A skill-sheet may be perceived by the student as an exercise far removed from one's actual life because it doesn't emerge from the student's need. Students in Jean Dickinson's fifth-sixth multi-age classroom compared their previous work with skill-sheets to their current literature discussions grounded in their own questions:

Megan: I don't like answering other people's questions when I have my own.

Kate: When I answer my own questions, I know who I'm answering for. When I answer a teacher's questions, I don't feel like I'm answering for myself.

BJ: When a teacher gives us a question, they want a direct answer
          and we can't give them some of our own thinking 'cause that
          messes them up. Maybe those worksheets work better for teach-
          ers, but not for us.

These students have identified some important concerns with decontextualized activities. Giving students little opportunity to discuss halts their own
thinking and questioning. Also, implicit in skill-packs is a focus on one "right
answer." Many teachers remember looking at the worksheet and wondering
how the publisher got that answer! Yet, because it is in print, it must be right.
Children's creative and astute thinking is often disregarded in the name of
the "correct answer." Although skill-sheets may be easier for teachers and
helpful in keeping students busy, they don't always do what they claim because the students' goal is simply to complete them. Literature discussion,
on the other hand, opens up the potential of multiple perspectives on a story,
character, or event, and enhances the possibilities that students will explore
and examine different interpretations. A skill-sheet narrows the potential to
one right answer, while literature discussion opens the possibilities; a skill-
sheet imposes the agenda for reading, while literature discussion extends the
agenda.

Powerful literature study groups do not happen easily or quickly. They
need structure, planning, and procedures to encourage students to think deeply
and critically. Let us now consider how some teachers use procedures and structures to help make the groups powerful and to encourage more *skillful* readers,
writers, discussants, and thinkers.

Establishing a Context for Literature Study

The potential for dynamic literature discussion groups is enhanced when
the entire classroom is considered as a context for the study of literature. In the
following paragraphs, we consider three important contextual elements: using
talk as a tool for learning, supporting literature study with oracy and literacy,
and choosing books that are both supportive and illuminate life. All three aspects are necessary in order to establish a context for literature study.

Understanding Talking as a Tool for Learning throughout the Curriculum

Talk is an essential component in literature study. When teachers understand and value the power of talk to support learning, they are in a better position to establish structures and routines that will lead to productive, generative discussions. Through their talk, students shape and craft their own ideas,
take the ideas of others into consideration in order to modify their own, and
use talk as an aid to their thinking. As students have opportunities to work in
pairs and small groups, they use talk to enhance learning throughout their day.
As Barnes (1995) reminds us,

> Often we need to work to achieve new understandings, making connections
> with what we already know, trying out the new ideas in other contexts and for
> other purposes, testing whether other people "see" things in that manner, too.
> I once heard a teacher refer to it as "working on understanding." There are
> other media for working on understanding—writing, diagrams, and draw-

ings, mathematics and drama—but talk has the advantage that since it is flexible it enables us to change direction easily, to qualify our first thoughts, to reframe ideas in different ways, leap to new connections. Moreover, it is easily shared with others who may also be engaged in making sense of those experiences. (p. 3)

Students realize the power of talk while solving mathematical problems, figuring out cause-and-effect issues in social studies, or discussing a powerful novel in literature study groups. Small groups of people are engaged in exploratory talk that "aids the speaker, in collaboration with others to clarify and reshape ideas" throughout the day (Barnes, 1995, p. 4). Such exploratory talk leads to the dialogue that Peterson and Eeds (1990) explain. It is an opportunity for each student to bring a personal interpretation of the piece to the table, and, in collaboration with peers, create a meaning that extends each one's thinking. This collaboration through talk helps students forge new meanings that were not considered prior to the meeting. Through this dynamic interplay, students use literary elements, knowledge about the reading process, and insights about the book to craft new ideas.

Classroom Reading, Writing and Talking that Supports Literature Study Circles

Reading, writing, and talking throughout the day create the potential for deep discussions. Teachers read aloud often during the day and use the text to generate a discussion. The read-aloud selection may tie into the literature study, the theme unit, or inquiry study that students are exploring, or it may simply be a book that has been carefully chosen for the fun and delight of the language. Literature study starts here. Students share in the common experience of listening to a book with beautiful language, vivid illustrations, or a powerful plot. After the story is completed, the teacher may ask, "What did you think?" and then listen as students connect the world of the author with their own. Some teachers carefully choose multiple books from one author or illustrator to read aloud on progressive days and children begin to make fine distinctions about how characters change from one book to another, how the illustrations change, and how favorite characters or scenes appear in more than one book. Children begin to develop a reservoir of language to describe their responses to such books, and the language of literature that the teacher may use (words like *plot, character, setting, climax*, etc.) becomes their own as they use those words to converse with one another.

Likewise, in many classrooms the writing workshop time is closely coordinated with literature study. Talking about the craft of writing, listening to a read-aloud from a writer's standpoint, or engaging in a mini-lesson about an author's intention supports students as they read a piece of literature.

The teachers constantly demonstrate that literacy is important by reading themselves and talking to students about that reading. The time they pick for literature discussion and the regularity of the sessions signal to students that this is something important.

Selecting Supportive Books that Illuminate Life

We need to select books that help us to understand our lives, books that contain real characters that students relate to, books that show students a way life could be. Peterson (1988) states that we need books that "leave an essence of meaning behind." It is these meanings that students seize and discuss with one another, meanings that cause them to think and create deeper interpretations together. Once Carol was using a book that a friend had recommended because it was so humorous. The plot was a little vacuous, but it was a "cute book" and great for reading aloud. However, after talking about how "funny" it was, the discussion floundered—the students were stumped. The book lacked that "essence of meaning" that could illuminate their lives. The students quickly decided to read this book independently and choose another for literature discussion. Often when the discussion is scant and vapid we need to look to the book. We must choose books that demand that students think as they read or listen to the book being read aloud.

Within the context of literature study, teachers help students become more efficient, proficient, and skillful readers.

We also need books that support readers and the reading process while still having layers of meaning to engage students' discussion. Supportive Texts (Watson, 1997) are books that readers love so much that they are willing to work with the text in order to find the meanings. They aren't books whose readers know every word or understand every concept—they aren't "decodable text" (Watson, 1997). Nor are they books that one would use for guided reading, where the purpose is to learn strategies. Instead, they are books that grab children's attention and have structures such as predictable language, illustrations that enhance the text, or vocabulary that supports a child's efforts to create the meaning. Supportive texts are ones in which the child works with the author to mine the meaning.

Books that illuminate life and support the reader feel like old friends. One such chapter book is *The Music of Dolphins* (Hesse, 1996). This story documents the life of a girl, Mila, who has been raised by dolphins ever since a plane accident left her alone when she was three. At about age twelve, she is found by scientists and brought back to civilization. Hesse uses various print fonts and language styles to put the reader in Mila's place. The language that Hesse selects helps the reader consider the hard issue of removing a person from a foreign, but loving, environment to study the effects.

Illustrations that extend and enhance the meaning can also support readers. In *Storm on the Desert* (Lesser, 1997), students understand the size and importance of a saguaro cactus from the vivid illustrations of Rand. Lesser uses context to define difficult words, and predictability in her language choices, the events, and the characters in order to create this supportive text. Such stories resonate with children's experiences and support the reader's efforts to create meanings.

Care in choosing books is essential for students to get the most benefit from literature study. Besides choosing carefully, teachers must read the books beforehand. Teachers in literature-based classrooms are always reading. They are the ones who read children's books at soccer games, PTA meetings, and on airplanes. Summers are devoted to reading new books for next year. They know titles, authors, and illustrators and get excited when they talk about those "free points" they have spent on next month's book order.

Initiating and Maintaining Literature Study Groups

Often students and teachers new to literature study have no previous models or experiences on which to draw. For many, basal reading groups have been the expectation. Other students have had teachers who assigned stories to the whole group and then conferenced with students occasionally. These students may believe discussion means summarizing the plot as they might in a conference. They aren't sure what their teacher expects or what they should be doing when the teacher says "discuss." Eeds and Peterson (1997) maintain that it is "natural to talk about story and that we do so from birth" (p. 5). We agree, but believe that sometimes the "talking about story" is what children do at home or on the playground, but rarely in the classroom. Such real, honest talk seems out of place in many classrooms. Teachers can help students be more successful by making the structure of literature study explicit. For example, teachers who occasionally hold basal groups have them meet in the north corner at the kidney-shaped table, but hold literature study in the south corner on the floor to signal to students that the rules for literature study are different from the basal groups. Other teachers are quite explicit about the potential of a literature study group. They might begin the year by saying,

> We are going to be reading and discussing books. This is a lot like what you do when you see a good movie and just have to talk to someone about it. In our group, we won't need to raise our hands. Instead, we'll wait until the speaker has stopped and then add our ideas. We also will look at one another, not just me (the teacher). I think you'll find as we talk about these wonderful books that they connect to our lives and perhaps even help us to understand our own lives more fully.

Jean has found that clear student expectations for the literature discussion time are critical to the success of the literature discussion. Students know when in the daily schedule they will be part of the literature discussion groups and the procedures that they will be following in moving about the room and getting into their groups. They talk about the preparation they have to undergo to be ready for group discussion, and that they need to take with them their pencils, the novel, and their journals. Guidelines as simple as "no sharpening pencils, no going for drinks . . . no movement in the room during this time period" not only support the organization and format for this discussion, but also send the message that this is important work that we do without interruptions.

Early in the year, Jean asks students to engage in a fishbowl activity, in which each child gets an opportunity to model and to observe. Previously, Jean always started the year with the fishbowl, but she's realized that it can be more powerful after students have some experience with literature study. She explains literature study groups and asks five or six classmates to volunteer to be in a group that will model a discussion for the whole class. Often she chooses a novel that students have been reading, so that each child has his/her own book. She meets with the "model" students briefly and they discuss the guidelines for modeling a discussion. She asks them to have a journal entry ready, some ideas to share, and questions to ask. This group meets for fifteen or twenty minutes to plan for the next day.

Although skill-sheets may be easier for teachers and helpful in keeping students busy, they don't always do what they claim because the students' goal is simply to complete them.

The students in the fishbowl place their chairs in a circle in the middle of the room, while their classmates form a second outer circle around the fishbowl group. Jean asks for volunteers to be "anthropologists" and to note what their classmates talk about, what factors seem to move the discussion along and, in general, the responses to the discussion. They then listen as the volunteer group talks about the novel. Immediately following the modeled lesson, Jean uses chart paper to record the observations. She frames their responses within the context of "what went well" and provides guidelines that keep the feedback honest, but positive. Students in the past have listed such observations as "taking turns," "asking members to share," "revisiting the book," "asking questions about parts of the story that are confusing," "making connections to the other books they have read," and "plans for the next time they meet."

Jean makes sure that everyone has a chance to be inside and outside the circle, so that every student has a good idea of how literature discussion groups operate. Such careful and explicit demonstrations help students understand the expectations inherent within literature study. Often in the first few days after the groups have begun, she uses the "T-chart" to process with them how the literature study group went (Dickinson, 1993, p. 111). One side might be labeled "The discussion is good when," while the other might be labeled "The discussion lags when..." Thus Jean asks students to assume responsibility for working toward rich discussions. Using the charts and taking time to firmly establish the routine helps the students to be more independent and skillful in their discussions.

Giving Students Time to Read and Respond to Books

It is imperative that students have time to read. Students can read books silently, or aloud with a partner at home or at school. When students have time to read these books, they are able to make an individual response (Rosenblatt, 1938). They consider what the text means to them personally. They connect to the book and begin to build a repertoire of books they have liked, books with strong characters, good illustrations, scary endings, and so on. They begin to have favorite authors and illustrators.

Students can make a personal response in many ways. Some teachers ask them to place a post-it on a page or paragraph that was important and jot down why. Unlike the skill activity of locating the main idea, this strategy allows children to choose what to highlight. They may place a post-it to illustrate a connection from life to text or to mark a section with strong characters or vivid language that they wish to bring up in the group. Another way to initially respond is by asking students to use their journals to create an agenda of important ideas they want to discuss (Gilles, 1988). The agenda contains questions or issues that have been prompted by the text that students feel need to be discussed by the whole group. These ideas are often "why" questions. They may be certain vocabulary words/concepts that students didn't fully understand, or students may extend the story by talking about character motivation or author's intent. The value of the agenda is that it is the students' opportunity to wonder, hypothesize, and think on paper. They then can raise these issues with others who have read the book, but who have not created the same meaning. Such dialogue in the group furthers all the members' thinking.

Teachers who are worried about students' learning about and using the literary elements may wish to listen a bit more carefully as students talk about books. Students invariably talk about the most compelling parts of the book. Students who read *Tuck Everlasting* (Babbitt, 1975) or *Roll of Thunder, Hear My Cry* (Taylor, 1976) talk about the characters and the tough decisions that they must face, while students who read Paterson's *Jip—His Story* (1996), wonder about the cruelty of "poor farms." These books compel talk of character development, plot, setting, style, and a wealth of other literary elements. The talk in literature discussion that engages students in meaningful dialogue, pushes them to higher levels of thinking, and expects them to clarify their understanding of concepts can come only from literature that is rich in literary elements. The key to a meaningful discussion about literature is a story that tugs on the heart strings, raises emotions, and asks questions of the reader that are not easily answered.

Talking about Strategies

If enough trust has been built, students also talk about the strategies that they use as readers in literature study groups. Teachers can prompt such discussions by occasionally asking students, in a "mini-lesson," to note the kinds of things they do as readers to further their understanding. Their comments can be displayed on a large chart. This was the list of strategies generated last quarter by students in Jean's classroom:

Rereading
>   Because of distractions
>   I left out a word
>   The language broke down
>   I didn't get it
>   I liked the passage and wanted to reread

Read on to get meaning

Use my prior knowledge

Make connections to my own life, to other stories, to events in the world

I asked myself questions about who the characters are: which one is which

I wrote an emotional response to what a character did

I talked with friends about the stories
>   I get titles of good books from others

I visualize—see pictures in my head of what is happening

I predict

I know when I don't know; I know when I'm confused

I read on to prove or disprove the predictions

I monitor my reading speed

I go back into the text to reread earlier parts to confirm

I ask "I wonder" questions

I monitor the strategies being used

Such a list is interesting for a number of reasons. First, students are reporting that they are using the same skills that are contained in skill-packs—identifying characters ("knowing which character is which"), monitoring speed, rereading for a purpose, and so on. However, instead of *practicing* a skill in a decontextualized way, they are *applying* that skill as a way to create more meaning for themselves from the book. If they can apply it, they must know it. Also, these students are aware of and able to articulate the strategies that they use. They talk of monitoring their strategies and they know when to use them. They have considered reading rates, and know when to skim or read carefully. Addressing such issues explicitly helps students to be more metacognitive about their reading and to learn more about the reading process as they learn more about literature.

For example, seventh grade students labeled learning disabled were discussing *Old Yeller* (Gipson, 1956) with their teacher, Mr. Vandover. One student questioned the word "hydrophobia" in the book:

Vandover:	I'd like to go back to what you said. About rabies, do you think you could find that part?
	(Students look in text)
Dan:	I wasn't going to write it down, but I heard Joshua say, "What does that word mean?"
Joshua:	When they didn't say "rabies" before when I read it, I stopped there and I said, "What is this 'hydrophia?" I didn't read on. If I had read on, I would have found out. (Gilles, 1991, p. 238)

Note the kind of language these students who were labeled "learning disabled" used. They were concerned about words making sense in the context of the story. They knew that they could write them down and bring them up in the group. Joshua realized that he can read on to find more information and perhaps solve his problem. The strategies helped them have more meaningful conversations.

Students in Jean's class talked about the processes they use in the literature discussion groups:

Jake:	We make our own questions. We talk about the intense part in the Mildred Taylor books. You read the intense part and you tell someone about it. Two heads are always better than one.
BJ:	When we are reading the Mildred Taylor books, we are reading about the same family. We already know the characters. We can visualize them in the other books.
Brock:	We can figure out words and the story if we reread and talk about it.
Nina:	Yeah, we found some words that we didn't know, so we got the dictionaries.

These students use a number of supports to make meaning. They question based on their needs; they are not being asked questions driven by a need for a teacher to have a score or to cover a certain skill. They use the support of multiple books. Jean realizes that the text itself is a powerful teacher, so she encourages students to read more than one book from an author. In the Mildred Taylor books, characters are repeated, so students' backgrounds are enhanced as they read about characters in various situations. The books themselves become supports to students' understanding and critical reading. Again, they know strategies that can help them create meaning from texts.

The Role of the Teacher

How can the teacher be a support in literature study groups? Lauren Freedman, (1991) describes a teacher's role as being both a participant and a guide. As a participant, the teacher reads the books, jots down her own questions, and sets a tone of curiosity and excitement in the literature discussion group. The body language of the teacher can communicate eagerness, interest, and respect to each child who speaks.

As a guide, the teacher is constantly demonstrating the processes that one goes through in reading and writing. Jean likes to read aloud a favorite, such as *Tuck Everlasting* (Babbitt, 1975), and stop to comment in a natural, spontaneous way. As she reads, she gets involved in the story, and automatically stops and responds with comments, such as "I love that passage" or "Oh, here's something else that is a circle in the story," or "I wonder why Natalie Babbitt had the man wear a yellow suit?" Such questions demonstrate to students that reading is active, and that good readers constantly look for patterns and sometimes they find that their questions aren't easily answered.

As a guide, the teacher also helps students delve deeply into the book. One way to encourage deeper analysis is to think carefully about the books that one will be using, and arrange them in such a way that each one builds on the last.

Jean was interested in having her fifth and sixth graders read Mildred Taylor books. In order to help her students understand the culture of Black America in the early 1900s, Jean began reading *White Lilacs* (Meyer, 1993) to the class as a read-aloud. In addition, she read the picture book, *The Story of Ruby Bridges* (Cole, 1995), and encouraged students to watch the television video. All these books and talk about the books created more background that enabled students to delve deeply into Mildred Taylor's work and to understand the complex issues at the core. Likewise, Jean decided that students could read more than one Taylor book if they wished, so the books themselves helped them engage deeply.

A skill-sheet narrows the potential to one right answer, while literature discussion opens the possibilities; a skill-sheet imposes the agenda for reading, while literature discussion extends the agenda.

Teachers help students dig deeper in the books by posing "I wonder" questions or comments. These are new concepts that the teacher raises for students to consider. Smith and Edelsky (1990) call these comments "literary balloons," statements that spark students' thinking and debate. The questions need to be real for the teacher, or the teacher needs to pose an issue and then let students look for the documentation. For example, the teacher might comment, "Looking at the prologue of *Tuck Everlasting* (Babbitt, 1975), I noticed a lot of references to circles." The students, some of whom perhaps haven't noticed the symbolism of circles, suddenly do notice and begin searching for examples of symbolism. This process propels them deeper into the themes of the book.

Another way a teacher can act as a guide is to slow down the conversation when one student has discovered something exciting but no one else has noticed it. Then the teacher acts as a regulator, slowing down the conversation to make sure that the comment is heard and acted upon by the others in the group.

A teacher guides by using judicious written support for students. This does not mean a ream of handouts that ask a myriad of questions about the story. Judicious written support is an opportunity for students to extend their thinking by using paper. The writing activities are not an end-product and are generally not graded. The written activities are chosen based on what the teacher notices the students doing in the preceding days and what activities are needed to support their thinking. For example, if students are reading a difficult fantasy book and the characters are confusing to them, the teacher might suggest using a character web or creating an ongoing list of characters. On another day the teacher might suggest sketches, diagrams or artwork that would enable the students to experience the fantasy in deeper ways. Toward the end of the book, students might complete a form that helps them think about their progress in the literature study group. Judicious use means that the forms are used infrequently, as an addition to journal writing, and are often completed by pairs or groups of children.

Such guiding activities enable students to make their thinking explicit and move from a literal to a symbolic level. Unlike the skill-packs, they are based on the students' needs, intentions, knowledge, and questions.

A Challenge

The archaic meaning of skills according to Webster (1967) is *to make a difference*. We want our students to read, talk, and think so that they make a difference, so that they influence one another and find meaning and joy in the print that they encounter. We want them to make a difference in the ways in which they interact with one another and in the amount and quality of literature that they read. We want them to understand that individuals can make a difference, by putting into action a lesson they have just learned and talked about, and that like-minded people can surely make a difference at the polls or in a community project. We want them to be *skilled*, thoughtful, eager readers, writers, and thinkers. For these lofty goals we must look beyond the scope and sequence of skill-packs that are suffocating good literature. We must enable our students by knowing the structures and processes that make deep discussion possible and then by trusting the students, the literature, and the process.

References

Babbitt, N. (1975). *Tuck everlasting*. New York: Scholastic.

Barnes, D. (1995). Talking and learning in classrooms: An introduction. In C. Gilles & K. Pierce (Eds.), *Primary Voices K-6: Talking and learning in classrooms*, 3 (1): 2–7.

Cole, R. (1995). *The story of Ruby Bridges*. New York: Scholastic.

Dickinson, J. (1993). Children's perspectives on talk: Building a learning community. In K. Pierce & C. Gilles (Eds.), *Cycles of meaning*. Portsmouth, NH: Heinemann.

Eeds, M., & Peterson, R. (1997). Literature studies revisited: Some thoughts on talking with children about books. *New Advocate 10* (1): 49–60.

Freedman, L. (1991). Teacher talk: The role of the teacher in literature discussion groups. In K. Pierce & C. Gilles (Eds.), *Cycles of meaning*. Portsmouth, NH: Heinemann.

Gilles, C. (1988). Reading, writing and talking: Using literature study groups. *English Journal, 78* (1): 38–41.

Gilles, C. (1991). *Uses of talk in literature study by adolescents labeled learning disabled*. Unpublished dissertation. University of Missouri.

Gipson, F. (1956). *Old Yeller*. New York: Harper.

Hesse, K. (1996). *The music of dolphins*. New York: Scholastic.

Lesser, C. (1997). *Storm on the desert*. Ill. T. Rand. San Diego: Harcourt Brace.

Meyer, C. (1993). *White lilacs.* New York: Harcourt Brace.

Paterson, K. (1996). *Jip—His story.* New York: Dutton/Lodestar Books.

Peterson, R. (1988). Teaching about literature. Presentation at the CEL Conference, February 18–19. Winnipeg, Manitoba.

Peterson, R., & Eeds, M. (1990). *Grand conversations: Literature groups in action.* New York: Scholastic.

Pierce, K. M. (1990). Initiating literature discussion groups: Teaching like learners. In K. Short & K. Pierce (Eds.), *Talking about books.* Portsmouth, NH: Heinemann.

Rosenblatt, L. (1938/1965). *Literature as exploration.* New York: Modern Language Association of America.

Smith, K., & Edelsky, C. (1990). *Literature study: Karen Smith's classroom.* Video. Tempe, AZ: Center for Establishing Dialogue in Teaching and Learning.

Taylor, M. (1976). *Roll of thunder, hear my cry.* New York: Dial.

Taylor, M. (1975). *Song of the trees.* New York: Scholastic.

Watson, D. (1997). Talking about books: Beyond decodable texts—supportive and workable literature. *Language Arts, 74* (8), 635–643.

Webster's Ninth New Collegiate Dictionary. (1991). Springfield, MA: Merriam-Webster.

Webster's Seventh New Collegiate Dictionary. (1967). Springfield, MA: G. & C. Merriam.

Strength in Numbers: Professional Growth through a Collaborative Agenda

Patricia L. Scharer

During her presidential address at the National Reading Conference, Kathryn Au (1997) provided an historical overview of pendulum swings common to the field of literacy. This time, she warned, it's different. For the first time, the decision-making powers concerning literacy instruction are centered in state and federal legislative mandates designed to control reading instruction and reading research. At the state level, mandates include required phonics courses for all preservice and inservice teachers, bans on specific types of reading materials in favor of "decodable" texts, and restrictions limiting inservice professionals to only discuss the use of graphophonic cueing systems. At the national level, every major literacy professional organization (NRC, NCTE, IRA, and NCRLL) opposes the federal Reading Excellence Act, objecting to its restrictive definitions of reading, reading instruction, and reading research.

Headlines proclaim the "Reading Wars," pitting whole language against phonics. The once-heralded California Reading Initiative is denounced as a failure despite the presentations of David and Yvonne Freeman (1997) and Charlotte Huck (1998), who have identified other factors that may account for the recent drop in test scores in that state, such as large class size, insufficient school libraries, poor teacher preparation, and the large percentage (40%) of uncertified California teachers.

The current back-to-basics movement has been criticized for relying on irrelevant research (Allington, 1997; Routman, 1996), denying the complexities of teaching and learning in favor of simple solutions and intruding on the opportunities students have to read quality literature and to write for sustained periods

Patricia L. Scharer is an Associate Professor in the School of Teaching and Learning at The Ohio State University at Lima where she teaches courses in children's literature and literacy instruction.

(Freeman, Freeman, & Fennacy, 1997). Clearly, the current political climate and level of legislative mandates demands a rapid, powerful response from teachers, supervisors, and administrators who understand the contribution of literature-based instruction to children's education. Because there is strength in numbers, this response needs to be collaborative and not just individual.

For the first time, the decision-making powers concerning literacy instruction are centered in state and federal legislative mandates designed to control reading instruction and reading research.

In this article, I first propose the need for teachers, supervisors, and administrators to form a partnership as learners to study themselves, their students, and the political agenda to create a unified response to the concerns of parents and legislators. Next, I suggest the potential for a collaborative study of alternative assessment tools to document student learning, not only to inform instructional decisions but also to document student achievement. These propositions combine to support educators during their quest to provide quality literature-based literacy instruction within a challenging political context.

The recommendations proposed are based on data from four studies in a series of research studies my colleagues and I have conducted over the past eight years employing a variety of methodologies (Gill & Scharer, 1996; Scharer, 1992a, 1992b, 1995; Scharer & Rogers, 1994). Although the researcher's lens was focused largely on teachers, classrooms, and children in each study, the school administrator consistently emerged as a significant factor in the findings. Thus, I will use the voices of both teachers and administrators across these studies to argue for a collaborative agenda with important instructional implications.

Mutual Needs of Teachers and Administrators

In separate studies, teachers and administrators have expressed identical concerns about literacy education. A national random survey of 581 elementary public school principals identified the top three unresolved literacy issues as whole language versus basals, assessment of reading progress, and the use of children's literature instead of basals (Jacobson, Reutzel, & Hollingsworth, 1992). Similarly, 84 teachers who attended a regional children's literature conference described the challenges they experienced as they struggled to document student progress without basal worksheets or unit tests and create literacy lessons with limited materials (Scharer, 1995).

During a nine-month case study of five teachers who were moving away from the use of basal reading materials toward a literature-based approach, additional difficulties emerged (Scharer, 1992a, 1992b). First, teachers were concerned about their limited knowledge of children's literature. Cullinan (1989) writes with regret that teachers may not have taken a children's literature course in 10 to 15 years, thereby limiting their instructional decisions. Similarly, the teachers in this study found it difficult to match books with the needs and interests of their students or to find quality books about specific topics for thematic studies given their limited knowledge about recent books.

A second concern arose while planning for instruction without using the prescribed sequence of teaching suggestions from the basal manual. For the first time, the responsibility for selecting the materials, sequence of lessons, and instructional strategies shifted to the teacher, causing increasing levels of discomfort. Teachers began to question the ways they were talking with students about their reading, the contributions of art and drama extension projects, the types of books they provided for students to read, the effectiveness of small group work that raised the noise level of the room, as well as the most appropriate way to document and assess student progress.

All of these concerns point to the need for educators to have the time and opportunity to increase their knowledge about children, reading, and books to more effectively accomplish programmatic changes. Smith (1997) argues that educators must "constantly examine their teaching and engage in some kind of systematic inquiry to make sense of what they want to understand" (p. 26). Data from the survey and case study research described above offer insight into ways teachers, supervisors, and administrators might find mutual support to diminish these concerns.

Collaboration Supporting Mutual Needs

Data analysis of the teacher survey (Scharer, 1995) revealed a small number of teachers (9%) who specifically recognized and appreciated the efforts of supervisors and administrators in response to the open-ended question, "What/Who has helped you use literature in your reading program?" For these teachers, supervisors and administrators provided important support as they worked together to implement a literature-based curriculum.

The year-long case study research project of five teachers in transition from basals to literature-based literacy instruction provides more specific insight into potential ways teachers and administrators might find mutual support (Scharer, 1992a, 1992b). Periodic interviews with the five teachers and the building principal, coupled with transcripts of after-school discussions with the rest of the staff, yielded important suggestions for supporting the professional development of educators.

First, both the teachers and building principal noted that talking with their colleagues during regularly scheduled small group meetings (called focus sessions) contributed to their professional growth. During a final interview, the principal commented that

> The focus sessions have been great. It gave [us] support from an expert in the field who could clarify things. Everyone got a lot out of it.

Recognizing the social nature of their learning was also evident as teachers credited attendance at children's literature conferences and visits to other schools as significant learning experiences.

Such opportunities, however, may be limited within the everyday schedule of the typical classroom teacher or principal, because interactions with other educators are often confined to brief encounters in the hall or rushed lunches in the lounge. Building-level collaborative meetings might take the form of monthly book clubs that explore professional books, children's literature, and other resources. The school's parent organization might support such meetings by providing a light breakfast or snack for those attending. The building staff could determine a specific topic for focus discussions and read pertinent articles, use audio or video resources, or invite guest speakers to inspire reflective conversation at such meetings. Small groups of educators who attend local, state, and national conferences or visit other districts could lead sharing sessions with the rest of the staff upon their return. Some suggestions can be accomplished with limited funds by building on the willingness of the staff to meet before or after school. Other, more costly activities could be funded through grant-writing efforts at the local, state, or national levels.

All of these concerns point to the need for educators to have the time and opportunity to increase their knowledge about children, reading, and books to more effectively accomplish programmatic changes.

A second type of professional support emerged from this study and resides at the classroom level. At the end of the nine-month study, teachers consistently identified my presence in their classes and the focus on implementing a literature-based approach to language arts instruction as supporting their personal growth. During the final interview, Andrea, the sixth-grade teacher reflected:

> Just focusing on it [literature-based reading] has helped us to learn more about it, explore our feelings about it, and explore what we want to do. It has made us look at ourselves more in depth than we would have. It has given us a chance to reflect and figure out where we want to go and given us some courage to try the move in the directions that we want to go. It has been the reason I have moved as much as I have.

For an entire school year, I was an active participant in five elementary classrooms. I did not assume the "fly on the wall" stance of the detached researcher but, instead, became a regular participant in the lives of the teachers. Classroom observations were not made from the back of the room but, rather, as a participant in the activities of the day. Interviews with each teacher five times during the year were opportunities to talk about their current issues, concerns, challenges and celebrations and collaboratively plan ways to try new ideas.

For example, during an early interview, Andrea wondered how to conduct book discussions with her students that are not simply oral worksheets with the teacher firing one question after another. Together, we planned to explore this issue by dividing the class in half so that she could talk with a smaller group about the survival novel they were reading while I met with the rest of the class who had been reading a different book. We each agreed to make every effort to participate in the conversations without dominating them. After listening to tapes of each other's conversations, we concluded that listening to students' responses and questions about books without the threat of teacher-made questions could reveal important information about students as readers. This event was the beginning of Andrea's attempts to organize book discussion groups in a variety of ways for the rest of the year.

There were other times when teachers asked questions during interviews or observations and I responded by providing professional readings. After reading an article about differences between good readers and poor readers, Nadine, the special education teacher, reflected:

> We tell a kid if they don't know a word, slow down [and sound it out]. In those articles that you gave me, it says that that's probably not correct. The better readers go faster. If you slow down, by the time you get to the end of the paragraph, you will have forgotten the beginning.

This article, coupled with Nadine's attempts to take running records (Clay, 1993) while individual students read, helped redefine her role from having students struggle to sound out words or telling them the word to documenting the strategies students used while working on unknown words and teaching additional strategies to help them become independent readers. For Nadine, reading and discussing a relevant article and learning a new assessment tool was a powerful opportunity for professional growth.

I also modeled lessons for younger readers with over-sized books (often called Big Books), inviting children to read along and attend to the features of the text. At other times, I demonstrated assessment techniques, provided books to match the instructional level of a child, suggested books for thematic planning, and worked individually with students at the request of teachers to identify areas for instruction and suggest appropriate reading activities and materials.

The role I played was a coaching one; providing personnel to serve in such a role requires some flexibility, creativity, and a high level of cooperation. One possibility is to redefine the role of a teacher with a strong background in children's literature and literacy to teach students each morning and work in other classrooms in the afternoon to provide the type of support described above. Every teacher in the building, however, can have the opportunity to observe and coach in another classroom if released by other school personnel. For example, supervisors, principals, or curriculum coordinators might videotape the lesson they teach while releasing the regular classroom teacher to observe or model a lesson in another classroom. The videotape could then become the focus of an after-school discussion of teaching strategies led by participating teachers.

The challenges facing each school building and district are unique and depend heavily on policies and personalities. The suggestions above are meant to serve as possibilities and ideas to be considered within the unique context of individual situations over an extended period of time. Solutions to these challenges may require commitment at the district level through sufficient financial support to not only acquire books and materials but also to provide release time for teachers and support for administrative staff looking to redefine an already challenging work load. Time, then, is not only a critical factor for teachers, but for administrators as well. Given increased national and state mandates that require mountains of paper work, challenging discipline problems, and constant public relations needs, further changes in the administrator's role may require that priorities be reorganized to secure adequate time. Possibilities include shifts in job descriptions, strategic use of volunteers, or the creative use of existing personnel.

Each of these suggestions requires dedication to the collaborative nature of learning and offer a variety of benefits including continuous professional growth and development of a unified building philosophy. Both better position educators to respond to local, state, and national mandates that require educators to clearly articulate their positions and philosophies.

Assessment: A Topic for Shared Inquiry

The voices of educators from the survey and case study research have been used to argue for the necessity of collaboration to satisfy mutual needs. Data from both studies revealed that the most frequently cited difficulty revolved around assessment. Consequently, this topic is proposed as a beginning for shared inquiry with the potential for supporting informed teacher decision-making, greater student achievement, and alternative methods for documenting student achievement. The voices of teachers from the case study research (Scharer, 1992a, 1992b) and teachers from a later study who examined their students' spelling achievement (Gill & Scharer, 1996) will be used to illustrate the potential of collaborative inquiry about assessment.

As teachers moved away from heavy reliance on end-of-level basal tests and worksheets, they became concerned about the assessment tools most appropriate for documenting student achievement and ways to translate such assessments into grades (Scharer, 1992a, 1992b). Teachers were also confused by mixed messages such as the challenge for creative, student-centered teaching and the ever-looming threat of accountability interpreted through standardized test scores (Gardner, 1988). Consequently, the tensions between authentic assessment at the classroom level, grading practices, and state or district standardized testing posed important challenges for teachers and administrators. Nadine, the LD teacher, for example, remarked,

> I guess the main thing I am worried about is the accountability. If a parent says to me, "Why did my child go from a C to a B in reading?" I need to be able to say, well, I listened to him read and I can see that he is progressing. But, I need something to back that up.

Without the easily graded worksheets and percentage scores from basal tests, teachers began to question their ability to document student achievement to support both grading decisions and lesson plans reflecting student needs.

Although uncomfortable about redefining grading practices, teachers tried new methods of assessment (i.e., anecdotal records, portfolios, conferencing, running records) and started to see students in new ways they found quite exciting. Nadine, for example, began to use running records (Clay, 1993) to document students' oral reading behaviors. (Running records are a type of short-hand used to record all oral reading behaviors while listening to a child read. When completed, accuracy percentages can be calculated and errors analyzed to gain insight into the strategies children use while reading. They also form a permanent record that can be analyzed over time for evidence of student achievement.) At first, much of Nadine's concentration was focused on writing the appropriate words and marks to record the student's reading. Gradually, however, the opportunity to listen to her students read individually, analyze the running records, and compare them over time enhanced her instructional decisions in an important way:

> When I first started doing running records, I just took them. Then you say, "OK, what am I going to do with this?" This has been a slow process for me. It has been overwhelming for me. Little by little, I am catching onto it. Oh, look what this kid is doing. He has done it in the last four running records. We need to work on that.

For Nadine, the opportunity to learn how to do running records and her restructured classroom organization which enabled her to listen to individuals read, had important implications for instructional change.

A later study focused on teachers' changes in terms of spelling instruction (Gill & Scharer, 1996). In response to questions about their students as spellers, teachers learned to analyze student spelling errors within a developmental perspective using an assessment tool called the QIWK (Qualitative Inventory of Word Knowledge). (See Schlagal [1989] for procedural details.) The QIWK is a series of word lists containing increasingly complex spelling patterns related to developmental stages. Children's attempts were first analyzed by calculating the percentage of correct responses for each list and then by examining errors for evidence of an understanding of word knowledge. Again, analysis of pre- and post-interviews with nine teachers revealed that the opportunity to look at student work in ways beyond right or wrong answers deepened teachers' understanding of their students and caused teachers to make important instructional shifts based on student needs.

Before using the QIWK, one teacher reported, "My kids were pretty close to the same . . . at a third- and fourth-grade level." As she used the QIWK, however, she learned that some students were functioning at a much lower level, causing her to reconsider the level of difficulty for instruction. Teachers' new knowledge of students based on the QIWK also affected their responses to student writing. Rather than circling spelling mistakes, teachers began to document patterns of errors in students' writing assignments in a systematic way that was informed by their work in analyzing errors from the QIWK. Consequently, teachers learned about their students as spellers and documented their achievement during the completion of various written assignments as well as within more formal spelling assessments.

Interactions with other educators are often confined to brief encounters in the hall or rushed lunches in the lounge.

Guskey (1986) argues that changes in teacher beliefs will occur only as a result of both changes in classroom practice and changes in teacher observations of student outcomes. If no changes are observed in student outcomes, classroom practices will be abandoned. Data from these studies suggest that learning new assessment tools may serve the dual process of reducing teachers' anxiety as they move away from testing with worksheets by providing important documentation to support grading policies, and may also positively affect changes in teachers' beliefs and instruction by enabling teachers to better see important changes in student achievement as a result of instructional change.

These findings call for the entire school staff to explore classroom-based, authentic assessment tools, value the time needed for collecting student information, and openly discuss findings relative to student achievement. The use of tools such as running records and the QIWK enabled teachers to see their students in deeper, more complex ways. Such knowledge is critical to planning instructional activities that meet the individual needs of learners and increase student achievement.

The Role of Mediation in Assessment

The documentation of student learning described above also offers the potential to support educators when challenged to define student gains in light of district or state standardized testing. Theresa Rogers and I explored the relationship between standardized testing and decision-making as part of a national study (Scharer & Rogers, 1994). Data collected in two urban alternative schools in a large metropolitan city included semi-structured interviews with two teachers in each building, multiple classroom observations in each room over a two-month period, and interviews with building principals, two students from each room, and two parents of children in each room.

Data analysis of teacher and principal interviews revealed patterns of tensions related to assessment, including concerns about the intrusive nature of standardized testing, dilemmas surrounding the manner and time of preparation for such tests, and the use of classroom-based assessments as documentation for letter grades. Both principals provided a variety of examples of how they mediate between the pressures of district-wide testing and their individual building philosophies.

At school B, for example, the test scores were viewed in a holistic manner in order to paint a larger picture of the data presented. Rather than examine scores at the level of the individual child or grade level, the staff at school B viewed scores in terms of patterns they have discovered over past years:

> We expect our 2nd grade children not to be as good in their reading scores as those people with the basal readers. The basal reader is just like climbing a ladder. They just go straight up that ladder. We are building out. They are going up the ladder and learning skills. They ought to do well. Our kids are lagging along and we're having a good time and know that we are going to finish in the middle of the pack [at second grade]. (Principal B, Interview)

His "ladder" metaphor continued as he described the scores at the grade five level:

> At fifth grade, it is a different story. The city wide test scores start falling off. The ladder goes up so high and it starts teetering. In fact, kids get up so high and they miss something or they have no data to cling to or they do not have a personal involvement in their reading. They are starting to have problems and the walls start falling down. Our kids are starting to come on. They are hooked into this and they have been choosing literature and things they are interested in. We have caught them on fire…[By fifth grade] our test scores are typically two, three years above the national average. (Principal B, Interview)

For this principal, viewing test scores in a global manner enabled his staff to avoid overreacting to initial low scores, secure in the belief that their philosophical stance would provide the children in their school with a wider ladder on which to base their learning. This principal served as a mediator to shelter teachers and students from excessive pressures related to standardized testing as teachers created classroom experiences consistent with each building's philosophy. He reasoned that the school is allowed to function with a minimum of pressure from the top due to the general perceived competence of the students as reflected not only in test scores but also observations of their performance, particularly after the elementary years:

> They are always surprised when our kids are able to do the things they are able to do and that they are so articulate and so equipped with vocabulary. They are stunned that after our kids leave our school they do so well in middle school and high school. It is just like shock after shock after shock. They can sit there and are begrudging to give us credit. It just goes on and on and on. It is kind of ridiculous. (Principal B, Interview)

At the district level, principals can mediate the pressures resulting from standardized testing by lobbying with other administrators to schedule the bare minimum number of district-wide formal tests. The manner in which such test results are analyzed will also have important implications for teachers. Building-level collaborative study can support such efforts by creating a unified philosophy and a stronger shared knowledge base about student progress documented through a variety of assessment tools.

Facing Challenges Together

The challenges facing education today need not be faced by individuals alone. The tendency for educators to work in isolation must be reshaped to include, support, and even require collaboration among teachers, supervisors, curriculum coordinators, and building principals. Collaborative inquiry about assessment tools is timely, given the current political climate, but topics need not be limited to achievement and testing. Opportunities to study and reflect on the role of quality children's literature in an integrated curriculum, how to develop parent/school partnerships, or the potential of technology within a literature-based curriculum offer similar advantages to educators. The responsibilities of educators are overwhelming at times. However, the potential contribution of the suggestions offered through the voices of teachers and administrators in the studies above must not be overlooked as a way to keep the pendulum moving toward a child-centered quality education for every learner.

References

Allington, R. (1997, December). *The "research synthesis" behind the phonics movement.* Paper presented at the meeting of the National Reading Conference, Scottsdale, AZ.

Au, K. (1997, December). *Transforming literature instruction: Reflections on recurring controversies.* Paper presented at the meeting of the National Reading Conference, Scottsdale, AZ.

Clay, M. (1993). *An observation survey of early literacy achievement.* Portsmouth, NH: Heinemann.

Cullinan, B. E. (1989). The national reading initiative: Outgrowth of the California Reading Initiative. *The New Advocate, 2,* 105–113.

Freeman, Y. S., & Freeman, D. (1997, November). *Helping teachers develop phonemic and political awareness.* Paper presented at the meeting of the National Council of Teachers of English, Detroit, MI.

Freeman, Y. S., Freeman, D., & Fennacy, J. (1997). California's reading revolution: What happened? *The New Advocate, 10,* 31–47.

Gardner, M. (1988). An educator's concerns about the California Reading Initiative. *The New Advocate, 1,* 250–253.

Gill, H. C., & Scharer, P. L. (1996). Why do they get it on Friday and misspell in on Monday? Teachers inquiring about their students as spellers. *Language Arts, 73,* 89–96.

Guskey, T. R. (1986). Staff development and the process of teacher change. *Educational Researcher, 15*(5), 5–12.

Huck, C. (1998). A letter to an assembly member. *The New Advocate, 11*(2), ix–xi.

Jacobson, J., Reutzel, D. R., & Hollingsworth, P. M. (1992, July/August). Reading instruction: Perceptions of elementary school principals. *Journal of Educational Research, 85,* 370–380.

Routman, R. (1996). *Literacy at the crossroads: Crucial talk about reading, writing and other teaching dilemmas.* Portsmouth, NH: Heinemann.

Scharer, P. L. (1992a). Teachers in transition: An exploration of changes in teachers and classrooms during implementation of literature-based reading instruction. *Research in the Teaching of English, 26,* 408–445.

Scharer, P. L. (1992b). Tensions between numbers and knowing: Changes in assessment during implementation of literature-based reading instruction. In N. D. Padak, T. V. Rasinski, & J. Logan (Eds.), *Literacy research and practice: Foundations for the year 2000* (pp. 3–13). Pittsburgh, KS: College Reading Association.

Scharer, P. L., & Rogers, T. (1994). *Assessment and decision-making in two schools: The Ohio site* (Tech. Rep. No. 596). Urbana-Champaign, IL: Center for the Study of Reading, University of Illinois at Urbana-Champaign.

Scharer, P. L. (1995). Making the move from basals to trade books: Taking the plunge. In B. Lehman & M. Sorenson (Eds.), *Teaching with children's books: Paths to literature-based reading instruction* (pp. 137–143). Urbana, IL: National Council of Teachers of English.

Schlagal, R.C. (1989). Constancy and change in spelling development. *Reading Psychology, 10*(3), 207–232.

Smith, K. (1997). A retrospective from the classroom: One teacher's view. *The New Advocate, 10*(1), 15–30.

The New Advocate

The Premier Journal for All Those Concerned with Young People and Their Literature

Call For Manuscripts

As editors of *The New Advocate*, we invite all those concerned with young people and their literature to submit articles about the difficult and complex issues surrounding the writing, publication, and teaching of this literature. We request scholarly articles that are of interest to practi-
tioners and practical articles that are grounded in current theory and research in language and
literature. We are especially interested in creative, yet provocative reflections on critical issues
and instructional strategies related to children's literature and its use in the classroom.

Sections of the journal include:

The Creative Process. This section contains lively articles and interviews by and about
active children's writers and illustrators and their work—the creative minds behind outstanding works. Past issues have featured pieces such as Jane Yolen's critique of current
trends in book publishing, Kathryn Lasky on writing outside one's culture, a conversation
with Cynthia Voigt, and Katherine Paterson on "family values."

Concepts and Themes. These refereed articles focus on current trends, recent research, issues of critical theory, genre studies, and other pressing concerns. Scholars featured in this
section have included Violet Harris on continuing debates and dilemmas in multicultural
literature, Ann Trousdale on a young girl's responses to feminist fairy tales, Charlotte Huck
on the history of literature-based reading programs, Maryann Eeds and Ralph Peterson on
revisiting literature study groups, and Gordon Pradl on literature and democracy.

Practical Reflections. Refereed articles in this section link theory to real classrooms and
share instructional strategies and practical ideas. Past features include Karen Smith on a
teacher's perspective of the literature-based movement, Vicki Zack on children's responses
to racism and genocide in literature, Rick Traw on responding to fundamentalist censors,
and J. Kevin Spink on children's responses to informational reading.

Learning through Story. At least one classroom vignette is published in each quarterly
issue of the journal. These stories, written by teachers and others directly involved in
schools, focus on students' engagement with literature in the classroom. Vignettes generally should not exceed 2–4 double-spaced, typed pages.

Children's Voices. Three to five children's responses to literature are published in each
quarterly issue of the journal. These responses take the form of children's written journal
entries, typed quotes, and/or artwork.

Letters to the Editors. We invite readers to respond to articles through Letters to the Editors.
Because articles in *The New Advocate* challenge our thinking by offering a variety of critical
perspectives on literature and teaching, readers may not find themselves in agreement with
the points of view of a particular author. We believe these points of disagreement offer the
potential for dialogue. We invite readers to write and become involved in the conversation.

<u>Manuscript Guidelines</u>. Articles generally should not exceed 20 double-spaced, typed pages. APA
style is preferred. Manuscripts are reviewed by at least two members of the Editorial Review Board.
Decisions about all articles are made within two to three months of submission. Include a cover
sheet with the author's name, affiliation, position, preferred mailing address, telephone number(s),
and FAX number. The author's name should not appear on the manuscript to ensure impartial
review. Please submit six (6) copies and two (2) self-addressed, stamped envelopes to: Kathy G.
Short and Dana L. Fox, Co-Editors; *The New Advocate*; Department of Language, Reading and Culture; 515 College of Education; University of Arizona; Tucson, Arizona 85721.

"I See My Father's Face . . .": Teaching Comprehension Strategies through Literature Study

Kathy Quick

Parker Palmer (1998) describes his best teaching as "moments in the classroom when I can hardly hold the joy" (p. 1). This is the story of one of those moments that occurred as I participated in a literature study group with fourth grade reluctant readers. This moment was a fusion of three critical elements: an extraordinary group experience, a text that taught itself, and an instructional model that met my students' needs.

Our excitement started with the group's choice of text. The participants (Emily, Britta, and Maya) selected the critically acclaimed novel *The Music of Dolphins* by Karen Hesse (1996). It is the story of Mila, a feral girl raised by dolphins, who is captured and studied by scientists. From the book's lead sentence, "*I swim out to them on the murmuring sea.*" (p. 1), to its closing line, "*I cover myself with my long hair, turn toward the soft blowing of my dolphin family, and give myself to sleep.*" (p. 181), we were hooked. This is a book that, in the words of Peterson and Eeds (1990),

> . . . invites all children into the world of story, first so they can lose themselves in it, and second so they have the opportunity to examine their responses in the company of other thoughtful readers—thus enriching their own understandings and perhaps finding some guidance in their own life stories. (p. 18)

The catalyst for our discussions usually came from my prompt, "What did you think or notice about what we just read?" At times, the girls' oral responses tumbled over each other in excited bursts. Not a disrespectful cacophony of sound–it was more like the collected voice of readers who were transacting with—their text on much deeper levels.

One particularly insightful moment came after reading about Mila recognizing herself in a mirror for the first time:

Kathy Quick is the language arts specialist for Breck Lower School in Minneapolis, Minnesota.

I am afraid. I was the girl with no clothes. I thought, This is a bad girl. She has no clothes. I saw her long wild hair. I thought, This girl is ugly with her long wild hair. (p. 107)

This excerpt led to a discussion of how females in our culture sometimes have negative physical images of themselves. Different perspectives were expressed. Maya remarked that when she looked in the mirror she hated the "fuzzy curly hairs" framing her face. But Emily stated proudly, "I *always* like what I see in the mirror!"

"Why is that?" we asked.

"Because when I look in the mirror . . . I see my father's face." My heart clutched as the group fell silent. Emily's father had died several years ago. She continued, "I like seeing my face in the mirror because it reminds me of my Dad. People tell me that I look just like him!"

Another profoundly personal exchange came from a discussion of who owns Mila: the sea, scientists, herself, and so on. This idea guided us toward the broader philosophical question of who really owns anyone. Emily exclaimed, "My mother owns me!" Britta retorted, "Not when you turn twenty-one!" Maya felt strongly that the government could own people. She explained, "My grand-parents were Russian Jews who were killed by the Nazis, so I think the govern-ment can own people."

My teaching objectives for this literature study were twofold: to interest these girls in a great book by an author whom they would hopefully continue to read, and to directly teach and practice key comprehension strategies with-out basalizing the literature.

The first objective was easy to meet due to the engaging nature of this text. As a resource teacher, I called this pull-out group a "Book Club." At our first meeting, we talked about what people do in Book Clubs. I described experi-ences in my two adult Book Clubs, and we munched on treats to build commu-nity. In addition, before beginning this novel, we watched CD/ROM movies of dolphins to build our background knowledge.

The second objective seemed more overwhelming to me. Was there a way to teach and practice comprehension strategies without destroying the enjoyment of the literature? Or . . . asked another way, could the head and heart of reading naturally coexist when using whole texts? I was anxious to find the answer.

In order to build the girls' repertoire of reading strategies, I needed to do two things: first, model what good readers do, and second, give them opportunities to apply their strategies in order to bring them to their conscious awareness. Routman and Butler (1996) write that "Having students articulate strategies they are just learning helps them to internalize and apply them in the future" (p. 5).

To accomplish these tasks, I chose the instructional model of "Thinkalongs" (Glazer, 1992). As I read aloud parts of the text, I described my thinking when using the strategies of predicting, asking myself "I wonder . . ." questions, vi-sualizing, making analogies, putting myself in the role of Mila, problem-solv-ing when stuck on words, rereading for better understanding, and summariz-ing. I also explained why I used certain strategies at particular times. The girls then brainstormed a chart of the strategies that they observed me employing. Eventually, we designed a "Thinkalongs Self-Monitoring Sheet" that would be used in later practice lessons (see Figure 1).

NAME _____   DATE _____

STORY/CHAPTER _____

THINKALONGS SELF-MONITORING SHEET

STRATEGY:	√ OR COMMENTS:
1. I PREDICTED <u>BEFORE</u> READING.	
2. I PREDICTED <u>DURING</u> READING.	
3. I ASKED MYSELF QUESTIONS (I WONDER . . . ?).	
4. I RAN A MIND MOVIE/VIDEO (VISUALIZATION).	
5. I MADE AN ANALOGY (THIS REMINDED ME OF . . .).	
6. I SAW MYSELF IN THE ROLE OF THE CHARACTER.	
7. I REREAD TO BETTER UNDER-STAND THE IDEAS/STORY.	
8. I REVIEWED USING THE 5 W'S: WHO?, WHAT?, WHEN?, WHERE?, & WHY?	
9. I USED THESE STRATEGIES WHEN "STUCK" ON NEW WORDS:	
• REREAD (BEFORE CLUES)	
• READ AHEAD (AFTER CLUES)	
• SOUNDED OUT LETTERS	
• LOOKED FOR WORD PARTS	
• SUBSTITUTED A WORD	
• USED A DICTIONARY	
• ASKED SOMEONE	
10. I SUMMARIZED AFTER READING.	

Figure 1. Thinkalongs Self-Monitoring Sheet

Adapted from *Reading Comprehension: Self-Monitoring Strategies to Develop Independent Readers* by Susan Mandel Glazer, published by Scholastic Professional Books. Copyright © 1992 by Susan Mandel Glazer. Reprinted by permission of Scholastic, Inc.

Volunteers read aloud portions of chapters. This was followed by discussion and tallying of the strategies that helped us to better understand the story. For example, after reading her portion aloud, Emily compared her section to a scene from a movie she had seen that week on TV. When asked what strategy she had just used, Emily answered, "I made an analogy!" In another example, Britta listened with eyes closed and a smile on her lips as I read aloud. Later, I asked her what she was doing. Beaming, she replied, "I'm running a mind movie video!"

My role shifted back and forth from group facilitator to group member. It was a delicate balancing act that allowed me to preserve the integrity of the literature and our personal responses to it, but at the same time, afforded me the opportunity to teach the important reading strategies these girls needed.

Even though Eeds and Peterson (1997) have cautioned about the danger of combining the teaching of skills with literature study group discussions, I believe this was the right instructional method for my students. It provided the scaffolding needed to help them grow into more strategic, independent, and engaged readers. And, it also gave me some teaching moments of pure joy!

References

Eeds, M., & Peterson, R. (1997). Literature studies revisited: Some thoughts on talking with children about books. *The New Advocate 10* (1), 49–59.

Glazer, S. M. (1992). *Reading comprehension: Self-monitoring strategies to develop independent readers.* New York: Scholastic Professional Books.

Hesse, K. (1996). *The music of dolphins.* New York: Scholastic Press.

Palmer, P. J. (1998). *The courage to teach: Exploring the inner landscape of a teacher's life.* San Francisco: Jossey-Bass.

Peterson, R., & Eeds, M. (1990). *Grand conversations: Literature groups in action.* New York: Scholastic.

Routman, R., & Butler, A. (1996). How do I actually teach reading now that I am using literature? *NCTE School Talk* 1 (3), 1–6.

**Special Thanks to Our Guest Reviewers
for Volume 11 of *The New Advocate***

Leslie Kahn
Tucson Unified School District
Tucson, AZ

Teresa McCarty
University of Arizona

Vicky Zack
St. George's School
Montreal, Quebec
Canada

Recommended

compiled by Shona McKellar

"A photographic, step-by-step guide to 29 traditional and contemporary fingerplays and rhymes for adults to share with babies and toddlers. With additional charming watercolor-and-ink illustrations accompanying these short verses, this collection will delight and entertain preschoolers." —*School Library Journal*

Illustrations by Priscilla Lamont.
Photographs.
PreK
ISBN: 0-7894-2861-X, $12.95

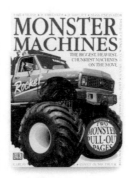

by Caroline Bingham

"In signature DK style—oversize, with plenty of pictures in color....Each two-page spread opens to one of the monster machines, which seems to be jumping off the page. It is surrounded by smaller photos and nuggets of information. Even though this is aimed at young kids, older students will probably be sneaking a peek, too." —*Booklist*

Photographs. Glossary.
Grades PreK-1
ISBN: 0-7894-2796-6, $14.95

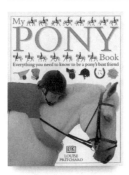

by Louise Pritchard

"...the world of the pony comes alive in this detail-filled volume. The author provides succinct, accurate information about the various breeds, their physical characteristics, history, and behavior....Excellent full-color photographs illuminate the text....informative and fun to read....A must-purchase." —*School Library Journal*

Photographs. Glossary, index, useful addresses.
Grades 3-7
ISBN: 0-7894-2810-5, $15.95

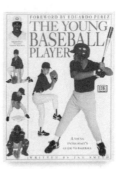

by Ian Smyth

"Brief chapters offer instruction on different aspects of the game mostly through captioned photographs. The inclusion of as many girls as boys in the illustrations is noteworthy. Smyth provides solid, basic information in an attractive format." —*School Library Journal*

Diagrams, photographs. Glossary, index, useful addresses.
Foreword by Eduardo Perez.
Grades 4-6
ISBN: 0-7894-2825-3, $15.95

DK Publishing, Inc., 95 Madison Avenue, New York, NY 10016
http://www.dk.com
Available from your regular supplier, or call 1-888-DIAL-DKP.

Children's Voices:

The journal entries featured here were used as touchstones in conversations in Tim O'Keefe's third grade class. They were bringing their intergenerational literature study to a close when Tim read *Sunshine Home* and a lovely new picture book entitled *The Sunsets of Miss Olivia Wiggins*. After reading both books back to back he gave the children time to reflect on the texts through writing. The children used their literature response to document connections, lessons, new insights, and important questions. After thinking through writing for approximately fifteen minutes, they all met to talk about the books.

Bunting, E. (1994). *Sunshine Home*. New York: Houghton Mifflin.
Laminack, L. (1998). *The Sunsets of Miss Olivia Wiggins*. Atlanta, Georgia: Peachtree Publishers, Ltd.

These two stories are really sad but I like the thing they thought of, they could of just picked something we do everyday.

I like the grandmother in *Sunshine Home*. She says "You know what, Tim? I'll trade it for a convertible. A red one." I thought that was really funny.

The other book called, *The Sunsets of Mrs. Olivia Wiggins* made me think of my great grandma. She lives in a nursing home too. She's really hard to understand because she speaks Spanish only, and even when she does speak Spanish it is only mumble. She is really happy to see me when I come, but doesn't know who I am. Well she does teach me Spanish because whenever she says something, my grandma (who usually takes me to the nursing home) tells me what it means. I always say to my great grandma, "Yo de keto mucho" which means I love you very much. She says in a trembling voice, "Yo de keto mucho domgaing" which means I love you very much also. It's sad when people get old timers (that's what my great grandma has).

By: Michelle Hinson

I think that books that can make you cry are the books that have really good sad descriptions. A good book sometimes makes you think in a different way.
By: Michael Huang

Responding to Literature

Sunshine Home
By Eve Bunting

This story really makes me think a lot about my grandma who died in a hospital and how things would have been.

The little boy in it reminds myself of me and how I was around my grandma.

It is a sad story that is so emotional and sad I wanted to cry.

It's stories like this one that really touch the heart and pierce you with sadness.

I also feel sorry for the boy because I too know what it's like to have someone close to you die. So in a way this story not only does good to me but to the people in the story.

And you shouldn't be scared to show your feelings. They are one of life's best gifts. Eve Bunting is now one of the best writers. She can experience love, and sadness, and hope. And to do that is one of the best things in the world.
By: Susannah Fields

These stories have a lot in common. They show how some children react to having their grandparents/great grandparents in a nursing home.

They remind me of my great uncle who is deaf in a nursing home and of my great grandmother who died because she caught on fire.

I wonder if Miss Olivia had some kind of memory/thinking disease. If she did I wonder what the disease was. It could have been Alzheimer's disease. This is a brain disease.

These stories are both very sad and serious. I wonder if any of these stories are based on something true.

I really like these kinds of emotional stories. The authors of these kinds of stories must be very talented because most authors aren't able to write stories that make people cry.
By: Rebecca Walden

Both of the stories are a wakeup call of how all the people feel. Like in *Sunshine Home* how Gram and Timmy's mom felt with sorrow and grief because they didn't share their feelings with each other. But when Timmy saw them cry when they were all alone, then Timmy brought them together to share their feelings. I think that made them feel like they knew each other much better. Like when we're in class and we write true or even sometimes fantasy stories, they make us feel like we know each other better. I like how the kids make a difference, them just talking about grownups. But at the end of the *Sunshine Home* it keeps you wondering.
By: Matthew Raley

"Reading the Word and the World" within a Literature Curriculum

Patricia Enciso, Theresa Rogers, Elizabeth Marshall,
The Ohio State University, and Christine Jenkins,
University of Illinois-Champaign/Urbana;
with Jacqueline Brown and Elizabeth Core, Indianola Alternative
Elementary School, Carmen Córdova, Worthington Schools,
Denise Youngsteadt-Parish, Neighborhood Services, and
Dwan Robinson, parent, Indianola Alternative Elementary School

If we are lucky, a book comes our way when we are young that affirms us, pleases us, satisfies us to the marrow and makes us reach for more. Many of us remember becoming readers through books that engendered this deep satisfaction while they also encouraged our awareness of diverse viewpoints and experiences. These books, and the adults who read with us, taught us, as Brazilian educator Paulo Freire described it, to read the word—and the world.

As new column editors, we invited a group of reviewers who would help interpret connections between books and the interrelated contexts of home, school, and community where children learn to read. Together, we have discussed our reading histories, our plans for this column, and the books to be reviewed. The childhood and adolescent literacy experiences of the review team are as varied as the reading materials we remember. We valued the kind of reading that allowed us to "savor the chapters," and reread "'til the pages fell out"—whether it was *My Side of the Mountain* (George, 1958) or the latest comic book. We enjoyed listening to parents' poetry recitations, overhearing dinner table book discussions, and escaping to secret places where we could read and avoid household chores. At the same time, we disliked school reading that included tests, "speed reading" lessons, and the bland texts that had little to do with our daily experiences. As is true for many children, the "real" work and

This column is edited by **Patricia Enciso** and **Theresa Rogers** with **Elizabeth Marshall**, The Ohio State University, and **Christine Jenkins**, University of Illinois-Champaign/Urbana. Review copies may be sent to: Theresa Rogers, *The New Advocate*, The Ohio State University, 216 Ramseyer Hall, 29 W. Woodruff Avenue, Columbus, OH 43210.

pleasure of reading occurred as part of the unofficial classroom curriculum or outside school hours. Fortunately, today's teachers work to recreate an "unofficial" setting for book talks and ongoing reading within the official reading and literature curriculum. These unofficial and official contexts for reading develop cultures or ways of noticing "what's in" and "what's out" as children seek validity among a community of readers.

We were impressed by the common experience of competition and judgment—for better or worse—that entered into our own and our children's and students' reading histories. Dwan said, "I remember last summer when my son was in a reading club through church and he got a trophy . . . because he just read so much. [It] wasn't until he did that and had the competitive thing going that he dug in and got interested." Dwan also noticed Jacob's eagerness to purchase a certain book at book fairs, "just because other kids in the classroom would have them." Liz added, "I have a really literate group of kids this year . . . and it [competition] worked in a positive way because . . . kids who weren't that interested in books have become very excited." Jackie referred to the social dynamics among children who select books that fit their image of being a reader. She observed that her third graders " . . . won't count *Nate the Great* (Sharmat, 1977) as a chapter book. It doesn't have the chapter numbers in it, even though it is like a chapter book. It doesn't count." No child likes to be left out of the community of readers whether it is due to the "look" of a book or the practice of learning to read separately from the group. Carmen remembered, "I was the only person in kindergarten that the teacher taught to read, and I hated that. She'd take me into a little room. I hated being separated out and doing that." Many of us also recalled the SRA kits that required us to use colored pencils and cards that clearly signified our place in a hierarchy of reading ability.

Like the children we teach, we could easily recall the ways reading literature was also a matter of reading one another. Children are interested in one another's perspectives but are also are sensitive to the ways they appear to be interpreted and represented by one another and by the books themselves.

Our reading histories provided a wealth of material for comparing and analyzing our own literacy development. A similar inquiry into children's unique reading biographies might offer insights for teachers, researchers, and caregivers as they try to understand the diversity of literary experiences and interpretations children bring into classrooms. A shared, deliberate inquiry into the ways children read the world of reading can provide important perspectives from which to build literature-based reading curricula.

As we introduce and review new children's books, we will present them within larger thematic frames such as "Re-presenting Gender Relations," "Understanding and Extending Kids' Favorites: Reading Literature with/against Popular Culture," and "Literature in the World: Stories of Social Activism." With the assistance of Christine Jenkins and the University of Illinois's Center for Children's Books, we will also provide historical information about books related to our themes which are considered "landmarks." Landmark books, discussed in each genre section, will help older readers and teachers deepen their understandings of the ways particular books have shaped and been shaped by the social and historical contexts in which they were written and read. In addition, these landmark books can help us talk with children about the enduring images and changing perspectives that affect our views of ourselves and others. Books that were, at one time, groundbreaking may seem rather mundane or even stereotypical to today's readers. On the other hand, many landmark books continue to raise perennial questions and highlight diverse perspectives through evocative, memorable characters, language, and images.

Each column will also offer a more lengthy review of a "feature book." Feature books are ones that we believe engender deep satisfaction with reading, while they also encourage our awareness and action on behalf of equity, diversity, and dignity in children's lives. Through this review we hope to describe the ways a notable book might help children read the word and the world. And so we begin.

Feature Book

Vera B. Williams. (1997). *Lucky Song.* **New York: Greenwillow Books. 28 pp. ISBN 0-688-14460-8.**

Vera Williams' newest picture book sings of the joys Evie seeks and receives from her loving family and the natural world. This is a book that will be loved by young children who recognize the pleasure of ready access to the goodness of the world. For older readers, Williams' understated narrative outlines the promise of our fundamental human rights: the right to a home, food, clothing, education, work, play, healthcare, and a clean environment. The endpages in primary colors move the reader from sunrise to sunset. Using her playfulness and insight with color, Williams shows Evie bedecked in yellow and orange against a muted indoor setting as she wakes and makes her plans, then heads outdoors where the strong angular lines of a green hillside challenge Evie's goal to run and fly her kite. Back at home, a tired Evie is welcomed with a hot meal, hugged by her sister, and serenaded by her father.

Climbing a hill, giving a meal, singing a song are simple acts and simple pleasures. But they are less simple for readers who know that even the most basic needs are not being met for thousands of children and families. Does Williams' story obscure the realities of woefully inadequate childcare, healthcare, and other social services in this country—and around the world? Reading this book in relation to the larger body of Williams' work, we find that, rather than obscuring the daily suffering of many children and families, *Lucky Song* reminds us of the promises made by legislators, families and communities to construct socioeconomic conditions that will make a full, cherished life a matter of fact, not luck. Evie's song can help children, teachers, and parents read the world as a hopeful, joyous place while they also consider the social conditions that are necessary to create safe, nurturing environments for more of the world's children. In this sense, Vera B. Williams, once again, gives us a vision that we can strive to turn into reality, together. *Lucky Song* is the recipient of the first Charlotte Zolotow Award sponsored by the Cooperative Children's Book Center in Madison, Wisconsin.

Many of the books reviewed in this, our first, column reflect the text and subtext of *Lucky Song*. *The Circuit: Stories from the Life of a Migrant Child* (Jiménez, 1997), *The Face at the Window* (Hanson, 1997), *A Pillow for My Mom* (Sgouros, 1998), and others describe the world through children's perspectives as they wonder about their relationships with their families, communities, and the land. These books also point readers to questions about inclusion and the meaning of community, labor conditions within and across U.S. borders, and the ways women contribute to strong, healthy communities. In subsequent columns we will continue to emphasize "reading the word and reading the world" as part of reading instruction in a literature curriculum, so that adults sharing books with children can consider ways they might reflect on the books we review in relation to the social conditions of children's lives.

Poetry: Surprising Words and Worlds

Although poetry has always been a comfortable form for some readers, we are aware that many children and adults shrink from its economy of expression and obtuse meanings. However, poetry need not be obscure or inaccessible, particularly when it is centered on the everyday moments and experiences in young lives. In fact, poetry can form the very core of a strong literature curriculum and reading program. We know from our own and our student's reading histories that humorous collections, such as John Ciardi's *You Read to Me, I'll Read to You* (1962) and Shel Silverstein's *Where the Sidewalk Ends* (1974) actually taught us to read. We also spoke of children in our homes and classrooms who loved Eloise Greenfield's *Honey I Love* (1972), and poems by Gwendolyn Brooks, Valerie Worth, Eve Merriam, Arnold Adoff, and David McCord. Poetry that is more familiar, humorous, or rhythmic invites eventual forays into poetry that is perhaps more difficult, more poignant, or more likely to change the way we see ourselves, others, and the world. The collections reviewed below include both sophisticated and more accessible works by a diverse representation of children and adults.

Francisco X. Alarcón. (1997). *Laughing Tomatoes and Other Spring Poems/ Jitomates risueños y otros poemas de primavera.* **Ill. by Maya Christina González. San Francisco: Children's Book Press. 32 pp. ISBN 0-89239-139-1.**

Winner of the 1997 Pura Belpré award for text and of an Américas Award commendation, Alarcón's poetry and González's bright, energetic illustrations capture the joy of living closely with the land and with the people who nurture earth's life. The fresh metaphors, based on the bounty of a spring planting, provide images of old and young people who are committed to the land and to the well-being of farm workers. Poems include a tribute to Cesar Chávez, and the delicate "Strawberries," a tribute to child farm laborers. Poems about songs, roots, tomatoes, and poetry itself make this a versatile collection for sharing with children across the year. Pat enjoyed hearing Alarcón talk about his poetry and the power of bilingualism for children at the Pura Belpré award ceremony. He delighted the audience with a reading of his opening poem, which requires the reader to turn the book upside-down, thus emphasizing the idea that "A poem makes us see everything for the first time."

Lori Marie Carlson. (1998). *Sol a Sol: Bilingual Poems.* **Ill. by Emily Lisker. New York: Holt. 32 pp. ISBN 0-8050-4373-X.**

As was done with Evie in *Lucky Song*, the poetry in this book follows the day of a thoughtful young girl as she describes the smells, sounds, and feelings shared by her family and friends, in the kitchen, the garden, on a hillside, and a sidewalk as they prepare food, dance, sing, and watch the day go by. Most of the poems were translated from English into Spanish, a difficult task that requires a feel for the expressivity and lyricism of Spanish as much as a knowledge of the language. Emily Lisker's use of strong contrasting color, pattern, and her loving characterizations of family and friends move the poetry's images into the reader's "mind's eye." As Carmen found when she shared this book with a group of bilingual and monolingual children, children's fascination with language and their capacity to communicate with multiple languages were extended and encouraged through this book.

Pat Mora. (1998). *This Big Sky.* **Ill. by Steve Jenkins. New York: Scholastic. 32 pp. ISBN 0-590-37120-7.**

Latina poet Pat Mora has written many books of poetry for children and adults, and is recognized as a strong voice in Latina literature. *This Big Sky* reflects her Southwestern heritage and her affection for the land, sky, and animals of the Southwest while poems set in the Midwest, her current home, remind readers that we are all living under one big sky. Mora's use of Spanish words, embedded in her poems, allow readers to quickly interpret their meaning while savoring the sounds of Spanish: *río, luna, lobo* and *Víbora*. Poems such as "River Sliding," "Noche," and "Halloween" will inspire children's writing, while the imagery and metaphors of "This Big Sky," "The Blue Door," and "Old Snake" can heighten children's understanding of poetic thought and form.

Naomi Shihab Nye. (1998). *The Space Between Our Footsteps.* **New York: Simon and Schuster. 144 pp. ISBN 0-689-81233-7.**

This book is an exquisitely produced anthology of poetry and paintings from the Middle East. The art, layout, endpapers, and indexes were carefully conceived to provide both a visual and poetic "feast of little dishes" with serious underpinnings. Over a hundred poems and paintings were selected from a call for entries to provide what Nye calls "deeper than headline news" about the people and life across the many and diverse countries that constitute the Middle East. The young adults with whom we read the book talked about their images of the Middle East and how these emanated primarily from popular culture where movies such as "Aladdin" reinforce stereotypes. They felt that this anthology provides a forum for discussing both negative and positive portrayals of Middle Eastern people. The young readers were puzzled by some of the poems and loved others. They were fascinated with the art and enjoyed talking about the varying styles represented throughout the book. Several poems stand out because of their accessibility for younger readers, their remarkable translations, and the way they speak to particular and universal human experience, including: "Rice Paradise" (Someck), a tribute to a grandmother's values; "The Strange Tale" (Al-Shabbi), a meditation on life and our future; and "Point of Departure" (Pagis) on the flight of imaginative writing.

Liz Rosenberg. (1996). *The Invisible Ladder: An Anthology of Contemporary American Poems for Young Readers.* **New York: Holt. 210 pp. ISBN 0-8050-3836-1.**

This is another finely produced anthology of contemporary American poetry for older children. In the introduction, Liz Rosenberg, the editor, argues that young people deserve great poetry, by which she seems to mean poetry written by "real" poets (such as Robert Bly, Allen Ginsburg, Maxine Kumin, and Alice Walker), not by "children's poets." This distinction betrays a bias against the very poetry that has brought many young children to an appreciation for humor, rhythm, and rhyme (by such notable poets as Judith Viorst, David McCord, Eloise Greenfield, and others) and a concern for only the most sophisticated young readers who are willing and eager to "break the code" of challenging works. Nonetheless, Rosenberg has put together an interesting collection of poetry with commentaries by each poet, and selected poems thought to appeal to older children or young adults. She has also included a useful section of ideas for encouraging young writers to write back—especially useful, perhaps, in poetry workshops and courses for teachers.

Many of the poets included pieces that are about childhood, or express childlike sentiments, but these are not necessarily what we found to be the most appealing works for young adults. The best poems are immediate, full of imagery, and moving. These include Galway Kinnell's poem, "Blackberry Eating," which is likened to writing in the lines: "the silent, startled, icy black language/ of blackberry eating in late September." Others that carry a sense of urgency or a questioning of justice (qualities that appeal to adolescents) include: "Barbie Says Math is Hard" (Mori); "Sterling Williams's Nosebleed" (Chin); "Who Burns for the Perfection of Paper" (Espada); and "Remember?" (Walker). This collection creates a new space for poetry collections that cross child/adult boundaries. Adult readers enjoying these poems can show children how to linger over poetry and help another generation reach for expressive language and startling images throughout their lives.

Davida Adedjouma. (1996). *The Palm of My Heart: Poetry by African American Children.* **Ill. by Gregory Christie. New York: Lee and Low. 32 pp. ISBN 1-880000-41-5.**

In the introduction to this collection of poems written by children and illustrated by Gregory Christie, editor Davida Adedjouma writes, "my interest in teaching stems from the belief that the gift of culture must be passed from generation to generation. . . . I hope this anthology will challenge other African American youth to explore creativity as a means of self-definition." These strong, clear, and moving poems were enthusiastically received by Jackie's second- and third-graders when they learned that children had written them. They noticed that words in the poems which are highlighted in bold-faced type are the most important words, ones that are also about being dark or black. These same words sometimes form interior poems, as in the lines: "**Black is** dark/ dark is lovely, lovely is **the palm of my heart**/and my heartbeats are filled with joy." As Lucille Clifton writes in the introduction, "Here dark is equated with wonderful and black with joy . . . lovely, indeed." We shared these poems with a fifth-grade girl who strongly identified with the themes of blackness and feminine strength. Although she struggled to read most prose, she read these poems eagerly and fluently, time and time again.

Ashley Bryan (Editor and Illustrator). (1997). *Ashley Bryan's ABC of African American Poetry.* **New York: Simon and Schuster. 32 pp. ISBN 0-689-81209-4.**

In this collection of African American poetry, Ashley Bryan draws on the alphabet as an organizing principle for introducing poetry and art to children. Whole poems from well-known poets and fragments of poems that stand on their own are presented for each letter and illustrated with stylized, richly colored paintings. Ashley Bryan writes in the introduction: "I worked from a list of over seventy African American poets. . . . As I read, images sprang from the lines of the poets and I began sketching . . ." The children who read this collection were excited when they recognized a poem and expressed an interest in sharing the tempera and gouache illustrations with their art teacher. Bryan invites young readers to seek out the entire poem and other works by these poets through a list of sources provided at the end of the book. Winner of the Coretta Scott King Award.

Picture Books: Imagining Words and Worlds through Visual Art

In literature-based classrooms and during library story times, picture books have long been the form most readily shared by adults and enjoyed by children. *Where the Wild Things Are* (Sendak, 1988) published more than thirty years ago is, without a doubt, one of the most widely read picture books. Teachers and children delight in the wild rumpus, and wonder at the absence of illustrations on the very last page. Many adults and children can recite the text by heart! However, at the time of its publication, many critics believed that the content was too frightening for children who might suffer from nightmares. In addition, the book seemed to suggest, much to many adults' consternation, that "being naughty" had its rewards.

It would be interesting to ask older students if they remember this book and if they think it might be enjoyed by younger children. Landmark books, such as *Where the Wild Things Are, The Very Hungry Caterpillar* (Carle, 1969), and *Brown Bear, Brown Bear* (Martin, 1983), are well-known by children and can be the basis from which they talk together about their memories of becoming readers and their interests in, and expectations for, picture books published today. Through their comparisons of older and current books, children can begin to recognize social and historical influences on the authors' and publishers' views of children; and they would certainly find, in their comparisons, that more books today reflect the diversity of our population. Yet, books that represent diversity are still limited relative to the numbers of books published annually in the U.S. And, although books published in the sixties and seventies began to reflect both greater diversity and a greater sense of realism, today's books, as we can see by the books reviewed here, are more likely to depict children's pain as much as their pleasures, their bewilderment as much as their insight, and their despair as much as their hope.

Charissa Sgouros. (1998). *A Pillow for My Mom.* Ill. by Christine Ross. Boston: Houghton Mifflin. 32 pp. ISBN 0-395-82280-7.

This spare and poignant story, gently illustrated with pencil drawings, begins, "My mom got sick this summer" and tells of a young girl's experience with her mother's death. It is effectively told in present tense although, as one young reader noticed on a second reading, the changing seasons of the drawings indicate the passing of a year. The young girl makes a pillow to ease her mother's and her own suffering, and is ultimately consoled herself by receiving the pillow back. Several children from diverse socio-economic backgrounds liked the book very much, although, as they said, "it is a sad story." As Denise pointed out, in poorer communities, death is more common and comes earlier. This book expresses for children, in a very simple way, the sadness they experience. Of the several books dealing with mothers and children that we reviewed for this column, this one seemed to us and to the children to be the most resonant and appealing. It would be a wonderful companion to *Everett Anderson's Goodbye* (Clifton, 1983).

Regina Hanson. (1997). *The Face at the Window.* Ill. by Linda Saport. New York: Clarion. 32 pp. ISBN 0-395-78625-8.

Regina Hanson says she wrote *The Face at the Window* because she is interested in mental illness and could not find a book for children that expressed the confusion children experience when they know or meet someone who suffers from these illnesses. Her story, set in her native Jamaica, describes Dora's fears and her parents' love as they begin what promises to be a cycle of care and inclusion for Miss Nella, the woman whose "face at the window" first frightened Dora. This rare story for children is beautifully told in a warm, Jamaican dialect that can be easily read aloud to children with a bit of practice. Linda Saport's illustrations capture Dora's fears and Miss Nella's hallucinations so that upper elementary children can comprehend the complexities of mental illness. Hanson and Saport also portray Dora's parents as loving role models who seek ways of opening windows and doors onto lives that are more often shut off from our view and compassion. *The Face at the Window* is a 1997 winner of the Américas Award for outstanding literature by and about children of the Américas. Hanson's first book, *The Tangerine Tree* (1995), is an Américas Award commended book. Both would be invaluable additions to a classroom or school library.

Participation Books: Making Words and Worlds Together

Many children's first experiences with literature and literacy occur as they interact physically and orally with books such as *Goodnight Moon* (Brown, 1947), *Brown Bear, Brown Bear* (Martin, 1983), *Baby Says* (Steptoe, 1988), and the books of Dr. Seuss. From choral reading to call-and-response, seek-and-find, and pop-up books, these books encourage shared talk and action that will help build a community of readers. The books reviewed below engage children with books through such activities as riddles, finger plays, and counting.

Valerie Bloom. (1997). *Fruits: A Caribbean Counting Poem.* **Ill. David Axtell. New York: Henry Holt. Unpaged. ISBN 0-8050-5171-6.**

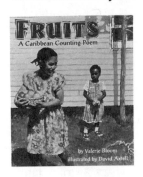

Valerie Bloom and David Axtell skillfully utilize the picture book format to create both a counting poem and a portrayal of two young girls growing up in the Caribbean. Dwan noted that the bright oil illustrations capture with striking verisimilitude the distinct colors of the region as well as the warm relationship between the two children. The rhythmic poem, written in dialect (e.g., "T'ree sweet-sop, well ah jus' might"), offers an opportunity to share and appreciate one manifestation of Carribean dialect. Yet, it also requires a sensitivity to the complex issues surrounding language and dialect. A thin line exists between language play and the use of dialect to reinforce and code derogatory representations. When read independently, written dialect may confuse emergent readers who are in the process of matching oral language with print. However, as a read-aloud or as a text for more mature readers, this book captures some of the richness of language variation among English speakers and provides opportunities for participation in reading, and counting for the youngest listeners, while introducing the fruits and culture of the Carribean.

Loreen Leedy. (1997). *Measuring Penny.* **New York: Henry Holt. Unpaged. ISBN 0-8050-5360-3.**

Loreen Leedy's latest addition to her series of math concept books features Lisa, who uses her dog Penny to complete a homework assignment about measurement. Jackie and other reviewers found it an excellent tool for introducing both standard and non-standard units of measurement, including time and money. Leedy's book is less a story than an instructional text, thus the book avoids a contrived plot. The text and illustrations are consistently creative, informative, and engaging. The book offered the children in Jackie's class an opportunity to play with math and invited them to share their own stories about dogs and other pets.

José-Luis Orozco (Selected, Arranged and Translated). (1997). *Diez deditos: Ten Little Fingers and Other Play Rhymes and Action Songs from Latin America.* **Ill. Elisa Kleven. New York: Dutton. 56 pp. ISBN 0-525-45736-4.**

This bilingual collection of finger rhymes and action songs from Spanish-speaking countries is selected, translated, and adapted by popular performer and songwriter, José-Luis Orozco. Orozco includes songs from several sources, including his mother and grandmother in Mexico City and families he met in Latin America and Spain while singing with the Mexico City Children's Choir. The songs and rhymes are colorfully illustrated by children's author/illustrator Elisa Kleven. Each song or finger play includes lyrics in both English and Spanish, an introduction to the piece and pictographs of the movements used when reciting or singing. Carmen read this book with children who talked about familiar cultural markers, and, like Orozco, recalled the people and circumstances surrounding the learning of particular songs and/or poems. The diversity of Latino/a culture is evident throughout the topics, songs, and language of this collection.

Brian Swan. (1998). *Touching the Distance.* **Ill. Maria Rendon. New York: Harcourt Brace. Unpaged. ISBN 0-15-200804-7.**

The creators of this book weave together Native American riddle poems and illustrations to create a sophisticated and interactive picture book. Through the use of poetic images, readers are challenged throughout to think metaphorically as they solve each riddle. The interactive nature of the book appealed to the fourth- and fifth-grade students in Liz's class who read it as part of a year-long study of North American Native history, stories, landscapes, and contemporary life. The students, who had a background in Native American story motifs, were able to guess many of the answers without looking at the pictures or checking the answers. They were intrigued by the illustrator's collages, which include combinations of wood, paint, and sculpture and are further embellished with materials such as cloth, eggshells, rocks, and clay.

Chapter Books: Engaging and Extending the Worlds of Older Readers

Whether or not classroom reading programs are literature-based, many teachers have read aloud *Charlotte's Web* (White, 1952), *The Little House in the Big Woods* (Wilder, 1953) and, in the last twenty-five years, Paterson's *Bridge to Terabithia* (1977) and Taylor's *Roll of Thunder, Hear My Cry* (1976). These books, now classics in children's literature, introduce children to characters whose dilemmas and desires are deeply felt and vividly expressed. Their literary quality and enduring themes have been applauded by children and by librarians and literary scholars who have named these titles either Newbery Award winners or honor books. All the members of our review committee had either heard or read these books, either as children or adults. Given the publication dates of these books and their constancy in home and classroom life, it is important for teachers to not only read the books for literary qualities and themes but to respond to the author's construction of characters' questions, agency, perspectives, misconceptions about and interpretations of the worlds they inhabit. Like the landmark picture books, these classics can be compared with contemporary titles that also feature strong female characters, close friendships, and perilous social conditions. One significant point of comparison may be between the pastoral ideal represented by earlier publications and the labor and lives of farmworkers and small community members today. Karen Hesse's *Out of the Dust* (1977), for example, radically alters adult and younger readers' assumptions of a comfortable rural life.

Francisco Jiménez. (1997). *The Circuit: Stories from the Life of a Migrant Child.* **Albuquerque: University of New Mexico Press. 134 pp. ISBN 0-8263-1797-9.**

Winner of the 1997 Américas Award, Jiménez's autobiographical novel portrays his family's journey from Jalisco, Mexico to California where they join "the circuit" of migrant families harvesting strawberries, cotton, and seasonal vegetables. As described in the Américas Award annotation, "The author poignantly weaves the family's customs, beliefs and hopes with the cruel reality of never-ending migrant labor camps from which escape is nearly impossible." Told from Francisco's viewpoint, the story includes episodes of schooling, notably the chapter "La Mariposa," which elegantly conveys the young boy's uncertainty and fears as well as his hopes for a better future. Indeed, La Mariposa is being produced by Houghton Mifflin as a picture book in the coming year. *The Circuit* fills a void in novels for young people. Its portrayal of a strong migrant family facing devastating social and economic conditions allows readers to begin to understand *la frontera*, the Mexican-American border, and the loss and promise of living and working in America's fields. This is a wonderful book to read aloud. Written with straight-foward, compassionate descriptions of migrant farmworkers' labor camp life, *The Circuit* will stir children to question the economic and immigration policies that place so many people in difficult living circumstances. It will be important to share related books such as *Calling the Doves* (Herrera, 1995), *Voices from the Field: America's Migrant Children* (Atkin, 1993), *Gathering the Sun: An Alphabet in Spanish and English* (Ada, 1997), and *Cool Salsa: Bilingual Poems on Growing Up Latino in the United States* (Carlson, 1994). *Boston Globe/Hornbook* Award, Fiction Winner, 1998.

Virginia Walter. (1998). *Making Up Megaboy.* **Graphics by Katrina Roeckelein. New York: DK INK; A Richard Jackson Book. 64 pp. ISBN 0-7894-2488-6.**

Virginia Walter's novel, a sixty-four-page compendium of perspectives, can be read in one quick sitting. However, all that becomes evident in a first reading is that thirteen-year-old Robbie Jones killed a Korean store owner; that Ruben was Robbie's trusted friend and Tara, his heroine; that his parents feel confused and betrayed; and finally, that Megaboy, Robbie's cartoon superhero creation, would be willing to risk his own happiness for the good of anyone in need, particularly children who are hurt and all alone. Each page of text, written as if transcribed from an interview, and the accompanying collage graphics, raise new questions about who knew Robbie and what could be known. The latter questions are the most pertinent for understanding the implications of a story told in such plain phrasing and limited imagery. Other novels for young readers have drawn on a variety of forms and styles (letters, interviews, alternating points of view, and a detached narrative reporting style) such as *Dorp Dead* (Cunningham, 1965), *A Hero Ain't Nothin' But a Sandwich* (Childress, 1973), *Nothing But the Truth* (Avi, 1991), and even *Maniac Magee* (Spinelli, 1990). In these novels, as in *Megaboy*, truth is impossible to grasp.

In terms of the relationship between the story's theme—that dangerously limited communication among key people in children's lives leads to disaster—and form, the novel excels. However, in terms of providing a well-wrought character, a carefully constructed sequence of episodes, and the elaborated insider perspectives typical of a novel form, this book fails. Readers are made responsible for extensively elaborating on the many gaps in the story. And that is, perhaps, the underlying rationale for the author's style and form; but it does not make it a fine novel. We worried about the ways younger readers and even adults might elaborate on the description of Ruben in the opening page of the novel: "He [Robbie] wasn't a bad boy. He didn't have bad friends, except maybe that Mexican boy who hung around for a while." Ruben is humanized to a certain extent across the book's pages, but not sufficiently to erase the derogatory power of these initial words. Although racism is an element of the unfolding perspectives and events, it is clearly left to readers to discern and imagine the relationship between racism and violence.

The timeliness of this story will surely make it a valuable part of classroom discussions about guns, youth culture, and adult responsibilities in our increasingly violent society. Sadly, current events actually diminish the power of this portrayal of youth committing horrendous acts of violence in their communities. And, like the evening news reports on the series of murders committed by children, *Megaboy* offers a reportage of events and artifacts, but little insight into the relationships and culture that engender these acts. We believe a reading of *Megaboy* will be strengthened by the shared reading of books such as *Scorpions* (Myers, 1988), *Staying Fat for Sara Byrnes* (Chris Crutcher, 1993), and *Parrot in the Oven: Mi vida* (Martinez, 1996), which allow children and adults to develop deeper empathy and understanding of the conditions and pressures that bring children into violent, devastating situations.

Nonfiction: Widening Our Lens on the World

Nonfiction literature has slowly but surely taken a more visible position in literature-based reading programs. With the work of authors such as Kathryn Lasky, Patricia Lauber, Russell Freedman, Milton Meltzer, and the ever-popular duo Joanna Cole and Bruce Degen of "Magic School Bus" fame, nonfiction is increasingly "readable" material for read-aloud times and small group book discussions. Well-written, carefully formatted nonfiction can become the first books children seek and cherish during their preschool, elementary, and middle school years. Alongside picture books and chapter books of related themes, nonfiction introduces children to intriguing, often suprising scientific, historical, artistic, and sociological perspectives on both familiar and distant worlds that would otherwise be interpreted through singular or superficial lenses. The four books reviewed here, all Américas Award honor and commended books, will invite children to become readers and to widen their views on both the diversity within Latino/a cultures and the similarities between families, sports fans, and gourmands across the Américas.

Margarita González-Jensen. (1997). *Mexico's Marvelous Corn.* **Illinois: Rigby. 16 pp. ISBN 0-7635-3182-0.**

Read with *Laughing Tomatoes and Other Spring Poems*, González-Jensen's brief but clear introduction to corn could become a classroom staple. She offers accurate Mexican vocabulary to describe, for example, the cornfields (*milpas*), corn dough (*masa*), and the sweet drink made with masa called *champurrado*. Clear photographs, food names, descriptions of food preparation, and a recipe for making tortillas create a highly accessible text for young readers and the adults who enjoy cooking and learning with them. This book, part of a Rigby series, is available in Spanish and English.

Patricia Almada. (1997). *From Father to Son.* **Photographs by Marianno de López. Illinois: Rigby. 16 pp. ISBN 0-7635-3133-2.**

The author and photographer of this book love sweet breads and cherish memories of eating these treats with family and friends. Readers will savor the pastries of the Montoya Pandaderia as they meet the Montoya father and sons and learn about a longheld family tradition of baking and selling sweet breads, first in the state of Nayarit, Mexico and now in Los Angeles, California. Children who are studying breads and foodmaking processes will be intrigued by the photographs of all the sweet bread shapes and designs created by the Montoya family in their daily work. Riddles at the end of the book will engage children in making up their own food-related guessing games. And the cost of producing 4,000 pieces of baked goods a day could become a centerpiece of several days' math calculations!

Henry Horenstein. (1997). *Baseball in the Barrios.* **New York: Harcourt Brace. 36 pp. ISBN 0-15-2004990-8; 0-15-200504-8 (pbk).**

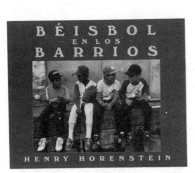

Fifth-grader Hubaldo Antonio Romero Páez proclaims that baseball or *béisbol* is Venezuela's most popular sport, thus making the game "an *all*-American sport—played in North *and* South America." Through Hubaldo's mediation, readers learn about Venezuelan schools, cities, and family life; however, we are primarily immersed in the world of baseball: famous Venezuelan players, teams, baseball cards, Hubaldo's team practices, hits and misses, and the tradition of the *madrina*—the team's godmother. Horenstein's narrative and photographs take us to formal and informal playing fields where bottle caps, broomsticks, and hard rubber balls often take the place of official baseballs and bats. A baseball glossary in Spanish and English at the end of the book helps young and older readers talk about the equipment, field layout, and other game terminology that is so familiar to fans and so confusing to novices. This book will make an important addition to a library's collection of fiction and nonfiction "baseball books."

George Ancona Mayeros. (1997). *A Yucatec Maya Family.* **New York: William Morrow. 40 pp. ISBN 0-688-13465-3.**

Many, many books are published each year that describe children around the world. Few measure up to the narrative quality and photographic insight of George Ancona's newest book. Ancona is of Mayan heritage and found, through this project, abiding connections between his family's traditions in Brooklyn, New York and those of the Yucatec Maya family of the Yucatán Peninsula. Armando, a young *Mayero,* and his family, descendants of the 4,000-year-old Mayan civilization, are the subjects of Ancona's description of Mayan life, past and present. One of the most remarkable aspects of this book—something that distinguishes it from books of this type—are the links he makes between a culture's rich knowledge and traditions and its contemporary, agrarian lifestyle. Through the inclusion of references to his own Mayan heritage, historical information, and reproductions of ancient codices alongside a strong narrative and warm, informative photographs, Ancona has redefined the standards for anthropological books for children. *Mayeros* is a 1997 Américas Award honor book.

References

Ada, A. F. (1997). *Gathering the sun: An alphabet in Spanish and English.* Ill. by S. Silva. Trans. by R. Zubizarreta. New York: Lothrop, Lee & Shepard.

Américas Award. (1998). <www.uwm.edu/dept/CLA/outreach—americas>.

Atkin, B. (1993). *Voices from the field: America's migrant children.* Boston: Little, Brown.

Avi. (1991). *Nothing but the truth.* New York: Orchard.

Brown, M. W. (1947). *Goodnight moon.* New York: Harper and Row.

Carle, E. (1969). *The very hungry caterpillar.* New York: Philomel.

Carlson, L. (Ed.). (1994). *Cool salsa: Bilingual poems on growing up Latino in the United States.* New York: Henry Holt.

Childress, A. (1973). *A hero ain't nothin' but a sandwich.* New York: Coward, McCann, & Geoghegan.

Ciardi, J. (1962). *You read to me, I'll read to you.* Ill. by E. Gorey. New York: Lippincott.

Clifton, L. (1983). *Everett Anderson's goodbye.* Ill. by A. Grifalconi. New York: Holt, Rinehart and Winston.

Crutcher, C. (1993). *Staying fat for Sara Byrnes.* New York: Greenwillow.

Cunningham, J. (1965). *Dorp dead.* Ill. by J. Spanfeller. New York: Pantheon.

George, J. C. (1959). *My side of the mountain.* New York: Dutton.

Greenfield, E. (1972). *Honey I love and other love poems.* Ill. by D. and L. Dillon. New York: Harper and Row.

Hanson, R. (1995). *The tangerine tree.* Ill. by H. Stevenson. New York: Clarion.

Herrera, J. F. (1995). *Calling the doves: El canto de las Palomas.* Ill. by E.

Simmons. San Francisco: Children's Book Press.

Hesse, K. (1997). *Out of the dust*. New York: Scholastic.

Martin, B. (1983). *Brown bear, brown bear, What do you see?* Ill. by E. Carle. New York: Holt.

Martinez, V. (1996). *Parrot in the oven: Mi vida*. New York: Harpercrest.

Myers, W.D. (1988). *Scorpions*. New York: Harper and Row.

Paterson, K. (1977). *Bridge to Terabithia*. New York: Crowell.

Sendak, M. (1963). *Where the wild things are*. New York:Harper.

Sharmat, M. W. (1977). *Nate the great*. Ill. by M. Simont. New York: Coward McCann.

Silverstein, S. (1974). *Where the sidewalk ends*. New York: HarperCollins.

Spinelli, J. (1990). *Maniac Magee*. Boston: Little, Brown.

Steptoe, J. (1988). *Baby says*. New York: Lothrop.

Taylor, M. (1976). *Roll of thunder, hear my cry*. New York: Dial.

White, E.B. (1952). *Charlotte's web*. Ill. by G. Williams. New York: Harper.

Wilder, L. I. (1953). *The little house in the big woods*. Ill. by G. Williams. New York: Harper.

Literature-Based Reading in Action:
Views from the Classroom

Myra Zarnowski and Karen Patricia Smith

As we begin our term as editors of this column, we would like to introduce ourselves and share our goals. We are interested in reviewing material for this column that helps educators integrate literature throughout the curriculum. Because of our past experience in elementary schools (Myra as a teacher, Karen as a teacher and principal), we value material that helps teachers with long-range curriculum planning—especially when that planning incorporates a great deal of literature. We also plan to review material that promotes a better understanding of children's and young adult literature. Both types of material are useful to us in our current work with preservice and inservice teachers (Myra) and with library media specialists (Karen). We look forward to providing *New Advocate* readers with information about resources that can serve their practical needs and promote their scholarly interests.

To complement the theme of this issue, we examine books that report successful practices in the teaching of reading within a literature-based curriculum—practices that invite passionate engagement with books and support students' talk and writing about the books they read. We discuss professional books that show what teachers are doing in their classrooms to make literature a vital part of children's lives.

Nancie Atwell's newly revised edition of *In the Middle: New Understandings about Writing, Reading, and Learning* (1998), invites comparison with the earlier 1987 edition. The new edition is not only noticeably larger; it is also significantly different. Drawing on her earlier work with adolescent writers, Atwell has now successfully combined both reading and writing into a single

Myra Zarnowski is a Professor of Elementary and Early Childhood Education and **Karen Patricia Smith** is a Professor of Library Science at Queens College of the City University of New York. Review copies may be sent to: Myra Zarnowski, Department of Elementary and Early Childhood Education, 65-30 Kissena Blvd., Queens College, CUNY, Flushing, NY 11367-1597.

workshop, one that "push[es] the parallels across the curriculum" (p. 36) in order to provide time, choice, access to materials, and opportunities for response and instruction. This is a welcome shift.

The book consists of three sections. Section One, "Always Beginning," deals with Atwell as a learner. She addresses how she has changed and modified her ideas about teaching reading and writing. Section Two, "Writing and Reading Workshop," the heart of the book, is a direct, nuts-and-bolts description of her work with seventh and eighth graders. Section Three, "Teaching with a Capital *T*," describes her rigorous, active stance as a teacher—one who not only models, but who also actively shows students what she knows about reading and writing. Here we see Atwell teaching about memoir, fiction, poetry, and persuasive writing.

Teachers will find many practical ideas related to the teaching of reading: numerous ideas for mini-lessons dealing with reading strategies, a list of 150 topics that apply to talking about books (derived from studying students' response journals), and samples of student journal writing. An updated and enlarged appendix section includes basic tools for setting up a reading-writing workshop: a reading survey, a student reading record, a listing of favorite adolescent literature, a list of favorite collections of poetry, recommended resources for teachers, and more. Teachers at all grade levels will find useful ideas about sharing literature with students, but perhaps more important, they will also find a memorable portrait of a teacher whose practice is based on careful observation of her students and thoughtful reflection about herself as a reader, writer, and teacher.

A well-rounded approach to literature-based instruction from the perspectives of twenty-five teachers and researchers is provided in *Literature-Based Instruction: Reshaping the Curriculum* (1998), edited by Taffy Raphael and Kathryn Au. Literacy instruction is viewed from the perspectives of theory, curriculum contents, literary selection, and assessment. Overall, the contributors make a substantial case for viewing literature as aesthetic practice worthy of study in its own right, which can also form the successful basis for the teaching of reading, self-understanding, and social action. The approaches offered are diverse. Violet Harris and Melodye Rosales in "Biracial and Multiracial Identity: Dilemmas for Children's Literature" discuss the debate regarding the impact of the role of race and ethnicity in the writing of literature, in historical and contemporary context. They emphasize, however, that while these are crucial areas which must be addressed, it is the excellence of the literature which ultimately determines the richness of the contribution. Au and Raphael in the essay "Curriculum and Teaching in Literature-Based Programs" emphasize the responsibility educators have to share with students the contents and components of literature, and how the reader responds to the message of the text. In Denyer and Florio-Ruane's "Contributions of Literature Study to the Teaching and Learning of Writing," the authors remind us that learning is not just for the young student, but for the teacher as well, a circumstance that may be theoretically self-evident, and yet is often overlooked in reality. An example is given of a student teacher who, in sharing Natalie Babbitt's *Tuck Everlasting*, learns much from the "conversations" of her students.

Given its wide-ranging presentation, the text has applications for undergraduate as well as graduate education students. It might well be of interest to those in the school media field, whose newly issued standards entitled *Information Power: Building Partnerships for Learning* (1998), place emphasis on literacy issues, primarily from an information retrieval and processing perspective. Since teachers and media specialists "share" the same students, it is crucial that both also share as broad a perspective of literacy as possible.

For those interested in promoting book discussion, *Peer Talk in the Classroom: Learning from Research* (1997), edited by Jeanne R. Paratore and Rachel L. McCormack, is an informative resource. As the editors clearly state, "The purpose of this book is to present classrooms where teachers have taken on the challenge to achieve a better balance in the talk structure of literacy lessons and have done so with notable success" (p. 2). And that is what they deliver.

An extremely useful first chapter entitled "'Do You Really Just Want Us to Talk About This Book?': A Closer Look at Book Clubs as an Instructional Tool" by Diane Lapp and her colleagues describes how to set up a book club program and assess student progress. The authors even suggest books to use and procedures to follow, and provide examples of response formats and writing prompts. Subsequent chapters show book clubs in action with different student populations—primary and intermediate grade children, ESL students, and struggling adolescent readers. In each chapter, authors provide many samples of student dialogue within peer-led groups. They succeed in showing that peer talk about literature is not only possible, but is a productive means of having students examine and refine their responses to literature. The samples are informative and inspiring.

Several chapters shift the focus from students to teachers, noting that teachers must do more than provide books and time for peer talk; they need to show students how to be effective participants. A final chapter demonstrates the benefits that occur when teachers observe peer talk in their classrooms and then use their observations to inform their teaching. Taken together, the chapters in this book effectively balance theory and practice to show the value of peer talk and how to get the most out of it.

Stephanie Harvey's *Nonfiction Matters* (1998) emphasizes the rich role that the study of nonfiction literature has to play in the development of information literacy and writing skills of young people. The role of questioning as "a door to human wonder" (p. 23) is underscored and also exemplified through numerous examples taken from the classroom. Such an approach gives credence to Harvey's case for nonfiction, and simultaneously assists both preservice teachers and veteran teachers in visualizing the interesting methods utilized by the author. Above all, the quality of the nonfiction to which students are exposed is the factor that determines the successful development of significant inquiry and learning.

Harvey suggests that when teachers share their interests with students and show how they find relevant information, this modeling behavior enables students to subsequently write more meaningfully. Such a "sharing" event also communicates the importance of what is being taught. Vehicles such as the "question web" stimulate information exploration and encourage students to engage in research. Harvey cautions against assigned research topics, and suggests instead that student interests form the basis for inquiry. Above all, she stresses that excellent and well-selected nonfiction literature serves as the ultimate springboard in assisting young people to read with the eye of a writer. Variety in print and non-print information tools, rather than over-reliance on the Internet, is recommended. The three sections of the book—"Conditions for Successful Inquiry," "The Nitty-Gritty," and "Putting It All Together"— allow the reader to comprehend the approach. This book, written in engaging text, includes both an extensive bibliography and an index.

When selecting literature to read and discuss, *United in Diversity: Using Multicultural Young Adult Literature in the Classroom* (1998), edited by Jean E. Brown and Elaine C. Stephens, offers up-to-date suggestions. This book consists of five sections. The first, "Listening to Authors," contains brief chapters by authors of multicultural literature for upper elementary and YA readers—authors such as Graham Salisbury, Joyce Hansen, and Christopher Paul Curtis. The authors wrangle with difficult issues such as whether writers can credibly write about cultures and races other than their own. These essays make for informative reading and are appropriate for sharing with students.

The second and third sections, "Connecting with Students" and "Expanding the Curriculum," consist of reports of how teachers in classrooms ranging from elementary through college incorporate multicultural literature study in their classrooms and integrate it across the curriculum. These teachers encourage their students to make varied responses to literature, including making portfolios and writing poetry and memoir. A particularly useful chapter by Kelly Chandler, "Considering the Power of the Past: Pairing *Nightjohn* and *Narrative of the Life of Frederick Douglass*," shows how a simpler book can serve as a scaffold for reading a more difficult one. In this case, *Nightjohn* provided a way into reading the more complex *Narrative*. Altogether, 15 chapters of ideas for connecting multicultural literature and classroom teaching are offered.

The final sections deal with issues related to multicultural literature—for example, the problem of "mentioning" rather than working toward in-depth understanding or the problem of selecting literature simply *because* of its ethnic content. The book ends with an annotated bibliography of multicultural books for young adults and a bibliography of resources for teachers. Teachers will find this a practical guide for using multicultural literature.

Poetry can form the basis for creative inspiration for young writers, and the poetry of other cultures offers the additional advantage of sharing a part of that culture with students. This is the case with *Luna, Luna: Creative Writing Ideas from Spanish, Latin American, and Latino Literature* (1997), edited by Julio Marzán. This bilingual approach presents rich examples of poetry from three cultures which introduce young people to poets often overlooked in mainstream texts. Marzán suggests that while "many teachers feel the need to use Hispanic writing because they have Hispanic students," in this book "the intention is to introduce students to models they can emulate in their own imaginative writing" (p. xii). Marzán offers examples of student writing in which young people were encouraged to draw upon images from the land of their birth. This is ultimately more effective in developing an appreciation for poetry than approaches to poetry from an analytical skills perspective. Dissecting a poem for its elements is immaterial or secondary to what the poem is really about. The editor also stresses the significance of background material on the poet in order to establish context and frame of reference. Marzán's poetic selections are filled with colorful images which can intrigue the senses of the reader. Using this book, teachers and students will have the opportunity to connect to the poetic past of Spanish speaking people from Spain and the Americas.

The books we have reviewed offer the unique insights of a variety of educators. While their approaches vary, each text presents a successful means of sharing books with young people within a literature-based curriculum. They each underscore the power of literature as an artistic form and its potential to influence perspectives, actions, and lives.

References

American Association of School Librarians, & Association for Educational Communications and Technology. (1998). *Information power: Building partnerships for learning.* Chicago: American Library Association. ISBN 0-8389-3470-6.

Atwell, N. (1998). *In the middle: New understandings about writing, reading, and learning* (2nd ed.). Portsmouth, NH: Heinemann. ISBN 0-86709-374-9.

Brown, J. E., & Stephens, E. C. (Eds.). (1998). *United in diversity: Using multicultural young adult literature in the classroom.* Classroom Practices in Teaching English, Vol. 29. Urbana, IL: National Council of Teachers of English. ISBN 0-8141-5571-5.

Harvey, S. (1998). *Nonfiction matters: Reading, writing, and research in grades 3–8.* York, ME: Stenhouse. ISBN 1-57110-072-5.

Marzán, Julio (Ed.). (1997). *Luna, luna: Creative writing ideas from Spanish, Latin American, and Latino literature.* New York: Teachers & Writers Collaborative. ISBN 0-915924-52-8.

Paratore, J. R., & McCormack, R. L. (Eds.). (1997). *Peer talk in the classroom: Learning from research.* Newark, DE: International Reading Association. ISBN 0-87207-181-2.

Raphael, T. E., & Au, K. H. (Eds.). (1998). *Literature-based instruction: Reshaping the curriculum.* Norwood, MA: Christopher-Gordon. ISBN 0-926842-70-6.

Additional copies of this special themed issue of *The New Advocate* (Volume 12, Number 1) are available at a cost of $14.95 each. Shipping and handling is $3.00 for one copy; 10% of total for two or more copies. Massachusetts residents please add 5% sales tax. Canadian and foreign orders will be billed for additional postage.

YES! Please send me _____ copy/copies of Volume 12, Number 1 of *The New Advocate*. I enclose $14.95 for each copy plus $3.00 shipping/handling for one copy; 10% of total for two or more copies.

Send to:

_____
Name

_____
Address

_____
City   State   Zip

How to Order:
* Call toll-free (800) 934-8322
  Please have MasterCard or VISA ready

* Fax (781) 762-2110
  Please include credit card information

* Mail to:
  Christopher-Gordon Publishers, Inc.
  1502 Providence Highway, Suite 12
  Norwood, MA 02062

The New Advocate

Payment Information:

__ Check enclosed
   (Payable to Christopher-Gordon
Publishers, Inc.

__ Signed school purchase order
attached

Please charge my:
__MasterCard
__VISA

_____
Card #

_____
Expiration Date

_____
Signature

Index to Volume Eleven

Title Index

Author Index

Yes! I want a student subscription to

The New Advocate

For Those Involved With Young People and Their Literature

- **Please enter my one-year student subscription (4 issues) starting with the next issue:**

  ❑ Check enclosed for $18.00 (prepaid subscription)

Send to.

Name _____

Address _____

_____

City _____ State _____ Zip _____

- All orders must be accompanied by check or money order.
- Prices are in US dollars and are subject to change without notice.
- Canadian and foreign orders will be billed for additional postage.

I confirm that I am a student and therefore eligible for this special rate.

_____   _____
                signature   date

Guarantee!
Full refund on the unmailed portion of your subscription, and on back issues returned in original, saleable condition within 10 days, if you're not completely satisfied.

Make check or money order payable and mail to:

The New Advocate
1502 Providence Highway, Suite 12, Norwood, MA 02062
(781) 762-5577

124321